ROYAL FLYING

A PICTORIAL HISTORY

KEITH WILSON

AMBERLEY

First published 2017

Amberley Publishing
The Hill, Stroud
Gloucestershire, GL5 4EP

www.amberley-books.com

ISBN: 978 1 4456 6494 1 (print)
ISBN: 978 1 4456 6495 8 (ebook)

British Library Cataloguing in Publication Data.
A catalogue record for this book is available from
the British Library.

Typeset in 9.5pt on 12pt Celeste.
Typesetting by Amberley Publishing.
Printed in the UK.

Contents

Introduction

There can be few readers who are unfamiliar with the Queen's Flight. Most will be able to recall seeing one of their bright red aircraft or helicopters at some time, be it in print or right in front of them. It is eighty-one years since the King's Flight was officially created back in 1936. Sadly, it is now twenty-two years since the Queen's Flight was effectively closed at RAF Benson and formally merged into No. 32 (The Royal) Squadron at RAF Northolt.

While No. 32 Squadron continues to operate at RAF Northolt, albeit in a much smaller way than it did at the time of the merger, it is not a dedicated Royal Flight, but provides VIP services to a range of users. Interestingly, most of the squadron's aircraft are capable of rapid conversion from VIP aircraft into regular trooping or cargo aircraft, or even for casualty evacuation. It is in this latter role that they have served so effectively during operations in Afghanistan and other theatres in recent years.

There is so much more to royal flying than just the King's Flight and the Queen's Flight. This book aims to demonstrate the long association that members of the Royal Family have had with aviation over the years and is more of a recollection of aviation-related activities undertaken by members of the Royal Family, including the more recent service activities by some current members.

The book features some of the earliest images of the Royal Family and their association with aviation – both of them taking to the air or reviewing aircraft on the ground. The oldest aviation-related image involving members of the Royal Family sourced during research shows a BE.2c of No. 4 Squadron performing a flypast at the King's Birthday Review at Ludgershall, near Andover, in June 1914. At the salute is General Sir Horace Smith-Dorrien, GOC Southern Command.

In *A King's Story*, the Duke of Windsor wrote: 'I had no desire to go down in history as Edward the Reformer: Edward the innovator – that might have been more to the point.' What so famously become the Queen's Flight was descended from the personal flying unit established by the Prince of Wales at Hendon in 1929, and which subsequently became the King's Flight under the Master of Horses' Department in 1936. This was as much an innovation as a means of royal conveyance, as was the motor car introduced by the earlier Edward.

However, Royal Flying may date back further than 1914. One document unearthed at the Queen's Flight Archive quoted a Ministry of Defence source as saying: 'The first flight by a member of the British Royal Family was made by Prince Leopold of Battenberg in January 1913, when he flew in a Bristol Monoplane with Howard Pixton at Madrid. However, his example was not followed until 1918, when the Prince of Wales was taken for a flight over the Italian Front.' Prince Leopold of Battenberg was, of course, a grandson of Queen Victoria; however, during research for this book, I have not been able to confirm the entirety of this statement.

What I can confirm, however, is that the first confirmed flight made by a member of the Royal Family was when Edward, the Prince of Wales – while on a visit to Villaverta on the Italian Front – was invited to fly in the rear cockpit of a Bristol F.2B Fighter with Captain W. G. Barker of No. 139 Squadron. Interestingly, the Prince remained standing in the rear cockpit throughout the short flight.

A month after his first flight in the F.2B Fighter, the Prince of Wales made a second flight with Captain Barker, this time in a civilian Sopwith Dove – one of the earliest sporting aircraft, with all the manoeuvrability of the wartime Sopwith fighter aircraft. Still recovering from his

The oldest royal aviation-related image sourced during research for this book shows a BE.2c of 4 Squadron performing a flypast at the King's Birthday Review at Ludgershall, near Andover, in June 1914. At the salute is General Sir Horace Smith-Dorrien, GOC Southern Command. (*Crown Copyright/ Air Historical Branch image H1671*)

A unique portrait of three British kings in Royal Air Force uniform. (*Crown Copyright/Air Historical Branch image H-483*)

wounds, and with his arm in a sling, Barker flew the Prince effectively with only one arm! On hearing about the risks involved, the King 'counselled his son not to fly again' – I believe this to be a polite way of saying 'you are grounded'.

Thankfully, the King's attitude to flying moderated and the Prince of Wales took to the air again on 27 April 1928. Once again, it was a Bristol F.2B Fighter and the Prince flew for thirty minutes in J8430 with Flying Officer G. C. Stemp of the Communications Flight of No. 24 Squadron at Northolt.

Just two weeks later, authority was received by the Communications Flight to increase their establishment of aircraft by the addition of one Bristol Fighter 'For Special Services'. This was the first establishment of an aircraft specifically for VIP purposes, although the precedent of

The author shares a humorous moment with HRH the Duke of Edinburgh during a visit to an aircraft company in North Yorkshire in 1998. The visit was made at the request of Buckingham Palace and the Duke arrived aboard Sikorsky S-76C helicopter G-XXEA. (*Via Keith Wilson*)

VIP aircraft had been set with the Communications Wing at Kenley, which was equipped with Handley Page 0/400 and DH4a aircraft for the carriage of delegates and despatches in connection with the Peace Conference at Versailles during 1919–20.

Later, the King's and Queen's Flight operated British-manufactured aircraft and flew them to all parts of the globe, thereby becoming a shop window for the British aircraft industry. Shortly after the King's Flight took four Vickers Vikings to South Africa for a Royal tour in 1947, which involved 160,000 miles of flight without incident, South African Airways placed an order for eight Viking aircraft.

As the title suggests, this is predominately a picture-led volume. In selecting the illustrations for this book I have often been obliged to choose between quality and originality. I have gone to great lengths to include as many 'new' images as possible. Where a poor quality image has been used, it is because I decided that the interest value of the subject matter warranted the decision, making it a better choice than a more familiar, previously published image.

Wherever possible, the source of the image has been acknowledged in the caption to each illustration. However, on occasions the widespread practice of copying images may have obscured the true origins of some. This may have led to some image credits in this book being incorrect. If this has occurred, it is completely unintentional and I do apologise.

I have thoroughly enjoyed researching this volume, the second in the new 'A Pictorial History' series for Amberley Publishing. I sincerely hope this book – reminiscing about Royal Flying in both words and pictures – enlightens and, more importantly, entertains the reader.

Keith Wilson
Ramsey, Cambridgeshire
August 2017

The Early Years

Edward, Prince of Wales, in the rear seat of a Bristol F.2B Fighter with Captain W. G. Barker of No. 139 Squadron during his flight in 1918, while on a visit to the Italian Front. (*Crown Copyright/Air Historical Branch image H1608*)

The first recorded Royal Flight can be traced back to 17 July 1917 when the Prince of Wales (later King Edward VIII) was taken up while in France. He enjoyed a thirty-minute flight above Abeele and Cassel in a Royal Aircraft Factory R.E.8. On 4 March 1918, Prince Albert was taken up for his first flight at the Royal Naval Air Station at Sleaford (later Cranwell), where he was serving as a naval officer.

The Prince of Wales' next flight was while on a visit to Villaverta on the Italian Front on 16 September 1918. He was invited to fly in the rear cockpit of a Bristol F.2B Fighter with Captain W. G. Barker of No. 139 Squadron. Interestingly, the Prince remained standing in the rear cockpit throughout the short flight. At the time, the Prince was a Major in the Grenadier Guards, serving on the staff of XIV Army Corps, and No. 139 Squadron was part of the Corps' air component. The Prince took another flight on 27 September, once again in a No. 139 Squadron Bristol F.2B Fighter, this time flown by Captain S. Dalrymple, RAF, and lasting fifteen minutes.

However, the Prince's very first flight in the Bristol F.2B with Captain W. G. Barker was to have serious consequences on his pursuit of aviation. A month after flying the Prince of Wales, Barker was promoted to Major and had been posted to the Western Front. During a dogfight in a Sopwith Snipe, Barker had been seriously wounded and was later awarded the Victoria Cross for his part in the event. Meeting the Prince of Wales in London after the war, he invited him for a flip in a Sopwith Dove – one of the earliest two-seat sporting aircraft, with all the manoeuvrability of the wartime Sopwith fighters. Barker, still recovering from his wounds and with his arm in a sling, flew with one arm. Upon hearing of the event, and the risks involved, the King instructed his son not to fly again!

Prince Albert Learns to Fly

Shortly after the war, Prince Albert took a flying course at Croydon under the instruction of Lieutenant W. A. Coryton. Two Avro 504s from the Air Council Communications Squadron were allocated for the task. Prince Albert received his wings on 31 July 1919 and on the following day his permanent commission to Squadron Leader was announced – making him the very first member of the Royal Family to become a qualified pilot.

Over the years King George V's attitude to flying mellowed and the Prince of Wales took to the air on 27 April 1928, once again in a Bristol F.2B Fighter III, although this time it was J8430 of No. 24 Squadron at Northolt, piloted by Flying Officer G. C. Stempe. Just two weeks later, authority was received by the Air Council Communications Squadron to increase their establishment of five Bristol Fighters, two Avro 504Ns and two de Havilland Moths by the addition of one Bristol F.2B Fighter annotated 'For Special Service', thereby creating the very first aircraft specifically for VIP purposes.

Westland Wapiti 1As Ordered

The allocation of the Bristol F.2B Fighter was purely an interim measure, pending the delivery of a pair of specially equipped Westland Wapiti 1s. Known in their new form as Wapiti 1As, these were standard production aircraft with the Scarff gun ring removed from the rear cockpit and then fitted out to VIP standards – although still retaining an open cockpit.

On 26 June 1928, the first of the two special Wapiti 1As – J9096 – arrived at Northolt, followed the next day by J9095.

First Solo Rivalry

Such was the Prince's interest in flying that in September 1929 he purchased his own aircraft – a de Havilland DH.60G Gipsy Moth, G-AALG. Following the acquisition, the Prince arranged for Squadron Leader Don to teach him to fly. Interestingly, George V raised no objections to this latest venture; such had been the change in his attitude towards flying.

At the time, the Prince's brothers – Henry and George (the Duke of Gloucester and the Duke of Kent respectively) – were also learning to fly and this led to some friendly rivalry as to who would be the first to fly solo. After several hours dual, Don sent the Prince of Wales solo during one summer evening. After successfully completing two solo circuits and landings, the Prince made a telephone call to report his success to his brothers.

The Prince used Wapiti J9095 on two occasions during 1929. On 10 September he was collected from Smith's Lawn at Windsor, which from around that time had become known as the Windsor landing ground, particularly after the erection of a windsock mast

On 5 June 1930, the Duke of Gloucester made his first official flight in an RAF aircraft when he visited Duxford in the Royal Wapiti 1A, J8096. However, when the Prince of Wales was asked to launch the new RNLI lifeboat *Sir William Hilary* at Dover on the same day, he chose to fly a No. 24 Squadron aircraft rather than the allotted Wapiti. This was the Hawker Tomtit J9772, which had been the first of its type delivered to the RAF. The new elementary trainer was a delight to fly and it would seem that it on this occasion Squadron Leader Don was the passenger! The Tomtit was landed at the old First World War airfield at Swingate, along the cliffs to the east of Dover.

'The Royal Flight' Moves to Hendon

Three aircraft – the Puss Moth and two Gipsy Moths – now belonged to the Prince of Wales; all operated under the supervision of Flt Lt Fielden at Northolt. Since the Prince held a nominal RAF rank, it was proposed that all three aircraft be transferred to Hendon, where they could be housed in the Display Hangar under the same conditions that permitted serving officers to maintain private aircraft.

The Prince was still carried in service aircraft from No. 24 (Communications) Squadron at Northolt but his private aircraft were transferred to Hendon late in 1930. Although not official designated – as they were still the Prince's private property – the term 'Royal Flight' was already being used, although it would be another six years before such a unit was officially established.

Buzzing the Royals

The Prince used Fairey IIIF K1115 on 13 August to visit a number of RAF stations during the Annual Air Exercises and suffered the first 'buzzing' of a Royal Flight. A squadron of patrolling 'Redland' aircraft in Armstrong Whitworth Siskin fighters spotted the Fairey IIIF cutting across their territory and, presuming it to be a 'Blueland' sneak raider, they promptly harassed it by simulating a series of attacks. The Prince, highly amused by the events, expected Squadron Leader Don to take evasive action but evidently he was not aware of the stringent orders the C-in-C Inland Area had laid down for the conveyance by air of the heir to the British throne.

First Amphibian Experience

In November 1930, the Prince flew in the world's largest heavier-than-air aircraft. Setting out from Hendon in Saro Cloud G-ABCJ and landing on Southampton Water gave him his first experience of an amphibian aircraft. Later, he transferred to the giant Dornier Do-X twelve-engine flying boat, and made a short flight sitting with the pilot. On returning to the cabin of the Saro Cloud, the Prince remarked: 'It's shrunk!'

There was a need for an aircraft larger than the three-seat Puss Moth. Interest centred on the Westland Wessex and the Prince had made a surprise visit to the Westland factory the previous year to examine the prototype. Later, when opening the airport at Roborough in July 1931, the Prince was flown back to London in Wessex G-ABEG. It was this aircraft that was loaned to the Prince for his tour of France along with a holiday at Cannes from 18 August to 19 September.

In 1932, in consultation with Flight Lieutenant Fielden, the Prince reviewed his fleet options. He decided to keep the two Gipsy Moths as sporting aircraft. The Puss Moth was useful, but rather cramped. However, the de Havilland Fox Moth, which had flown earlier that year, offered accommodation for four at the expense of a little over 10 mph in speed. The Prince decided to sell Puss Moth G-ABNN. In its place a de Havilland DH.83 Fox Moth was ordered, with G-ACDD being delivered shortly before Christmas 1932.

Vickers Viastra Ordered

Meanwhile, an important decision had already been taken on a larger aircraft for the Prince. This had been under consideration since chartering the Imperial Airways Wessex on several occasions, confirming the requirement of a larger aircraft capable of carrying an entourage and being a flagship for the Royal fleet of aircraft. Having carefully studied the market, Fielden recommended purchasing the Vickers Viastra, a type already proven in service with Australian Airways. A twin-engine version was required for the Prince and was designated the Vickers Type 259 Viastra Mk X. It was built in the Supermarine works at Woolston and registered G-ACCC. Before delivery, the aircraft was painted in the red and blue colours of the Brigade of Guards, in common with the Prince's three other aircraft.

de Havilland Dragon Ordered

The possibility of replacing the Viastra with a de Havilland DH.84 Dragon had been under consideration from as early as February 1933. A proposal had been made to the de Havilland company to swap the existing Puss Moth, Fox Moth and Gipsy Moth for a new DH.84 Dragon. After negotiations a deal was struck and Dragon G-ACGG was delivered to Hendon on 12 June 1933. It was finished with a red and blue fuselage, silver wings and red struts. It was first used just nine days later, for an official visit to Norwich, when the Prince flew into Mousehold Aerodrome.

When the Prince of Wales opened the present RAF College buildings at Cranwell on 11 October 1934, he flew there in the Dragon. In 1933, it was the best aircraft available on the market but by 1934 was being superseded in production by the DH.89 Dragon Six, later known as the Dragon Rapide.

In September 1934, Fielden commenced negotiations with the de Havilland company on behalf of the Prince. As the Viastra also needed replacing, Fielden was able to promise the purchase of two of the new DH.89A Dragon Rapides and the sum of £8,150 was eventually quoted by de Havilland for both. This expenditure was eventually offset by the sale of Dragon G-ACGC to Richard Shuttleworth at Old Warden.

Both DH.89A Dragon Rapide aircraft were required for delivery by May 1935, when an intensive flying programme was envisaged in connection with King George V's Jubilee celebrations. The first – G-ACTT – was delivered on 27 April, with the second airframe – G-ADDD – following on 8 June. However, little use was found for both aircraft and before the end of 1935 it was decided to dispose of G-ACTT – which had only flown for 51 hours since its delivery – and it was sold to Olley Air Services on 13 March 1936.

At this stage of proceedings, the Prince of Wales had only one aircraft and this was the position that prevailed when, in January 1936, the Prince of Wales became King on the death of Edward VIII.

Once he became King, he assumed the rank of a Marshal of the Royal Air Force and, as such, was entitled to aircraft for official occasions. The Air Ministry was responsible for funding the aircraft and agreed to meet the cost of one of the Prince's aircraft if used for official occasions. This, in turn, led to the formation of the King's Flight, which officially came into being on 21 July 1936.

On the same day, Flight Lieutenant Edward Hedley Fielden, AFC, was appointed as an Equerry in Waiting with the appointment of Captain of the King's Flight in the rank of Wing Commander. Up until this point, the salary of Fielden – the Prince's personal pilot – had been paid through the Keeper of the Privy Purse; however, he was promoted to the rank of Wing Commander to provide a status relative to his rate of pay, which was now to be paid by the RAF. Two civilian ground engineers – Theodore Jenkins and R. T. Hussey – were given RAF-equivalent non-commissioned ranks.

The Prince is seen standing up in the rear cockpit of a Bristol F.2B Fighter of No. 139 Squadron at Villaverta, Italy, in the summer of 1918. (*Queen's Flight Archives*)

HRH Prince Albert, who later became King George VI, was flown from England to France in a Handley Page O/400 bomber by Major Greig, RAF, on 31 October 1918. (*Queen's Flight Archives*)

Edward, Prince of Wales, and Prince Albert, later the Duke of York, seated together in a Handley Page O/400 bomber. (*Queen's Flight Archives image A038*)

Prince Albert gained his wings flying an Avro 504J, C4451, the first aircraft allocated specifically for a Royal task. (*Queen's Flight Archives*)

After the war, the Prince of Wales met Barker, now a Major with the Victoria Cross, and flew with him in a Sopwith Dove. At the time of the flight, Barker was still recovering from wounds received on the Western Front, and flew with one arm in a sling. When the King learned of the risks involved, he advised his sons not to fly again. (*Queen's Flight Archives*)

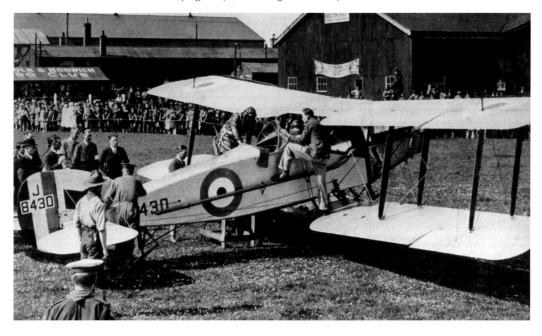

Bristol F.2B Fighter III J8430 was the first aircraft officially allocated for Royal engagements and was fitted with a specially modified rear cockpit. This image shows the Prince of Wales's departure from Mousehold Aerodrome on 30 May 1928. (*Queen's Flight Archives*)

HRH the Prince of Wales in flying kit and parachute.
(*Queen's Flight Archives*)

HRH the Prince of Wales seen climbing aboard an unidentified but beautifully polished Westland Wapiti 1A. Two specially equipped Westland Wapiti 1As were ordered and delivered to the Communications Flight of No. 24 Squadron at Northolt in June 1928 for VVIP flying. (*Queen's Flight Archives image A041*)

The first aircraft owned personally by HRH the Prince of Wales was this de Havilland DH.60G Gypsy Moth, G-AALG, which was delivered in September 1929. (*Queen's Flight Archives image A159*)

The Dornier Do-X twelve-engine flying boat D-1929 moored on Southampton Water in 1930, ahead of a visit from HRH the Prince of Wales. (*BAE Systems*)

The Prince of Wales inspecting the Dornier Do-X, a giant twelve-engine flying boat, at Southampton Water. The Prince had a short flight in the Do-X, which, at the time, was the world's largest heavier-than-air aircraft. (*Crown Copyright/Air Historical Branch image H2247*)

In 1929, the Prince of Wales chose Flight Lieutenant Edward Hedley Fielden as his own personal pilot. In this formal image, 'Mouse' Fielden is seen in his mess kit. (*Queen's Flight Archives*)

The Prince's first cabin monoplane was this de Havilland DH.80A Puss Moth, G-ABBS, construction number 2020. It too was painted in the red and blue Brigade of Guards colours. In 1931, on the first leg of a tour of South America, the Prince flew in G-ABBS to Le Bourget before taking a train to Santander, Spain, where he boarded the SS *Oropesa*. G-ABBS was flown back to the UK and sold. (*Queen's Flight Archives image A016*)

The Prince of Wales after arriving at Andover in Fairey IIIF F1115 during the 1930 Air Exercises. On the right is Air Vice-Marshal Sir John Steele, KBE, CB, CMG, AOC Wessex Area, who was commanding the 'Blueland' forces during the exercises. (*Queen's Flight Archives*)

The Prince of Wales photographed while inspecting Westland Wessex G-ABVB in 1930. (*Queen's Flight Archives image A024A*)

A three-engine, ten-seat Wessex, G-ABEG, was loaned to the Prince for his tour of France and holiday in Cannes from 18 August to 19 September 1931. In addition, the type was used by the Prince on a number of occasions during the early 1930s. (*Queen's Flight Archives image A024*)

Upon his return from the 1931 South America tour, this Armstrong Whitworth Argosy, G-EBLF *City of Glasgow*, was chartered to fly the Royal party from France back to the UK. At the time, it was the largest aircraft used for Royal Flight; it was also the largest aircraft to land on Smith's Lawn at Windsor. (*BAE Systems*)

Shortly before Christmas 1932, the Prince of Wales took delivery of de Havilland DH.83 Fox Moth G-ACDD. Once again, the aircraft was painted into the blue and red colours of the Brigade of Guards and followed the practice of Royal aircraft of having the last two letters of the registration the same. The smaller Puss Moth, G-ABNN, was offered as part-exchange in the deal. G-ACDD was later sold, in June 1935. (*BAE Systems*)

The first aircraft specifically ordered for Royal use was this Vickers Type 259 Viastra Mk X, G-ACCC, which was confirmed on 3 November 1932 at a price of £4,250. It was delivered on 16 May 1933 and the aircraft flew from Smith's Lawn to Cardiff and back to Hendon to present the Esher Trophy to No. 604 (County of Middlesex) Squadron of the Auxiliary Air Force. (*Queen's Flight Archive A019*)

Vickers Viastra X G-ACCC, showing the long-range tank fitted underneath the fuselage. Just visible in the background is the unusual three-engine Airspeed AS.4 Ferry, G-ABSJ, which was acquired by National Aviation Displays Limited. (*Vickers (Aviation) Limited via Queen's Flight Archive A524*)

A view of the interior of Vickers Viastra Mk X G-ACCC. (*Queen's Flight Archive A022*)

The Prince of Wales arriving at Brooklands ahead of a visit to Vickers (Aircraft) Limited. The pilot, A. H. 'Mouse' Fielden, is seen stepping out of the aircraft with engineer Tom Jenkins standing under the wing. The Viastra was sold in March 1935 after having flown fewer than 10 hours in the previous year. (*Queen's Flight Archive A520*)

The Vickers Viastra Mk X was little used and was soon replaced with this de Havilland DH.84 Dragon, G-ACGG, which was delivered on 12 June 1933. DH.60M Moth G-ABDB, DH.80A Puss Moth G-ABRR and DH.83 Fox Moth G-ABXS were all sold back to de Havilland in part-exchange for the new Dragon. (*BAE Systems*)

In 1934, the Duke and Duchess of York took their first flight together aboard a de Havilland DH.86 airliner. (*Queen's Flight Archive A021*)

An order was placed with de Havilland for a pair of DH.89A Dragon Rapide aircraft. The first, G-ACTT, was delivered on 27 April 1935. Once again, the Brigade of Guards colour scheme was favoured. G-ACTT did not serve for long and by October 1935 was being offered for sale, having only flown 51 hours. (*BAE Systems*)

King George V and Queen Mary visiting Mildenhall ahead of the England–Australia Air Race of 1934. Behind the Royal party is de Havilland DH.88 Comet G-ACSP *Black Magic* entered by Jim and Amy Mollison. Amy Mollison (née Johnson) can be seen to the right of the image. (*Queen's Flight Archive A522*)

The King's Flight 1936–39

One of the busiest days for Dragon Rapide G-ADDD occurred on 8 July 1936, when the new King, accompanied by his brother the Duke of York and the Chief of the Air Staff, visited several RAF stations in turn. The first call was at Northolt, where the Furies and Gauntlets of the resident Nos 1 and 111 Squadrons were inspected. (*Crown Copyright/Air Historical Branch image H1060*)

In early 1936, the Flight's single DH.89A Dragon Rapide, G-ADDD, was very busy. In addition to carrying the King, the aircraft was used by other members of the Royal Family and, in the latter half of 1936 alone, G-ADDD made sixty-one flights.

Its busiest day was on 8 July, when G-ADDD carried the new King, accompanied by the Duke of York and the Chief of the Air Staff, when they visited several RAF stations in turn. Their first call was to RAF Northolt, then RAF Wittering and Mildenhall. The final stop was made at Martlesham Heath, where the King was able to examine a number of new aircraft under evaluation. These included the Spitfire prototype K5054 along with the Hawker F36/34 monoplane, which later that day was given the name 'Hurricane' at an informal ceremony.

King Edward VIII Abdicates

The Air Ministry's offer to replace the Dragon Rapide from public funds was soon taken up. Once again it was Fielden's recommendations, but the King's choice of equipment. In addition to the Lockheed Super Electra, a wide range of British options were under consideration. However, before a final selection could be made, the King abdicated and the Duke of York acceded to the throne on 12 December 1936.

The new King – George VI – retained the services of Wing Commander Fielden as Captain of the Flight, but the Flight was without an aircraft. Dragon Rapide G-ADDD was still located in the hanger at Hendon and had already flown 194 flying hours; however, it was the personal property of the former King, now the Duke of Windsor.

Fielden was able to organise the sale of G-ADDD for £3,445 to Western Airways Ltd of Weston-super-Mare in May 1937, by which time a new aircraft for the Flight had arrived. Later, in June 1940, G-ADDD was impressed into RAF service and allotted the serial AW116. Sadly, like G-ACTT (X8509) before it, AW116 was struck off charge in May 1941 as 'damaged beyond repair'.

Airspeed Envoy

Early in 1937, interest had centred on the Airspeed Envoy. Despite the fact that Airspeed was a relatively new company, they already had a contract for the construction of 136 twin-engine trainers, a military version of the Envoy that would enter service as the Oxford. Arrangements had been made for Fielden to fly the Envoy at Christchurch on 3 March 1937.

Although he subsequently reported that he felt the Envoy was 'too small for the requirements of the Flight', it was the most suitable replacement for the Dragon Rapide. Fielden also suggested a number of modifications that would be necessary for its Royal duties and these were discussed with Airspeed's joint managing directors.

Specification 6/37 was issued to cover 'the Airspeed Envoy III aircraft for The King's Flight and to define certain special requirements which are necessary'. This was the first official specification to be made for a royal aircraft and the Airspeed Envoy, G-AEXX, was the first royal aircraft to be financed from public funds. The Envoy then had to meet the military requirements of the Air Ministry Directorate of Technical Development and Aeronautical Inspection, as well as satisfying the British Civil Airworthiness Requirements. In addition, the Envoy also had to satisfy the Captain of the King's Flight. These multiple standards have been applied at all subsequent peacetime acquisitions of aircraft for both the King's and the Queen's Flight.

The Envoy specification, 6/37, included a number of modifications, such as an enlargement of the cabin to include a radio and operator, which in turn entailed moving the bulkhead that divided the pilot's compartment from the cabin rearward by nine inches. Additional fuel tanks were installed in the wings and Fairey Reed metal propellers were fitted.

After delivery, the Airspeed Envoy was checked to specification at the Aeroplane & Armament Experimental Establishment at Martlesham Heath, before undergoing a series of test flights between 21 April and 3 May 1937. Once completed, the Captain of the King's Flight took possession of the airframe and engine logbooks... along with the key to the cocktail cabinet.

The Envoy was to be registered as G-AEXX, but was initially given permission to fly without the civil registration being displayed, although later the aircraft was suitably marked. No sooner than it had been, the Air Ministry decided they would supply and maintain the aircraft, and all servicing crew should be placed into uniform. Effectively, this meant the aircraft would actually be operated as a military airframe and the serial L7270 was allotted for the purpose. However, Fielden was unhappy with the views of the Air Ministry and tried to stall their introduction for as long as possible before the Air Ministry eventually agreed with his views and it continued to operate as G-AEXX.

The Envoy was soon busy. The King visited a series of RAF stations as well as a number of visits paid to aircraft factories meeting the increasing orders placed for the RAF.

Lockheed Hudson

When the war seemed imminent, it was decided that the King should have an aircraft capable of defensive armament. Following investigations, the Lockheed Hudson was chosen. A British Purchasing Commission had ordered 200 from the USA in 1938, which, at the time, aroused a storm of controversy. However, when war was declared, the order was increased and the Lockheed Hudson provided a valuable stopgap for Coastal Command, especially during the early years of the war.

Among the initial orders for the Hudson was a new aircraft for the King's Flight but by the time it was delivered, war had already been declared.

Next stop on the tour was at Wittering, where the Dragon Rapide was photographed arriving. After the King and his party left the aircraft, he was able to talk to trainees of the resident No. 11 FTS (Flying Training School). (*Crown Copyright/Air Historical Branch image H1059*)

HRH King Edward VIII arriving at Mildenhall on board DH.89A Dragon Rapide G-ADDD on 8 July 1936 to review his Air Force. (*Queen's Flight Archive A584*)

At Mildenhall, the King inspected the resident Handley Page Heyford IIIs of Nos 38 and 99 Squadrons, along with the Hawker Hinds of No. 40 Squadron. (*Crown Copyright/Air Historical Branch image H1549*)

In June 1936, the new King formally instituted the King's Flight. This immediately brought new status to the personnel of the Flight. On 9 June 1936, Chief Engineer Theodore Jenkins was enlisted into the RAF Reserve. The following day, he was promoted to corporal and later, on 22 June 1936, Jenkins was further promoted to the rank of sergeant. (*Queen's Flight Archive*)

31A

S.37623/P.3.,

9 June 1936.

Theodore Jenkins.

The Officer in Charge of Records,
Royal Air Force,
Ruislip,
Middlesex.

I am directed to request that the above-named whose present address is Newcastle Arms Hotel, Weybridge, Surrey may be invited to enlist into Class "E" Reserve in the trade of Fitter A.E.

Mr. Jenkins is in possession of Ground Engineers Licence A and C and is employed as Chief Ground Engineer to H.M. The King; trade test is therefore to be waived in his case.

Subject to Medical Fitness he is to be attested in the classification of A.C.2., and promoted the day following to the rank of Corporal.

I am to ask that this Department may be informed when attestation is completed.

A. S. ELLERTON.

Wing Commander "P" Staff,
for Director of Personal Services.

30th July 1936.

My dear Halsey

Thank you for your letter of the 10th of July in regard to the arrangements for The King's aircraft.

In accordance with His Majesty's wishes, I am arranging for Flight Lieutenant Fielden to be promoted to the rank and status of a Wing Commander in the Reserve of Air Force Officers. As to salary, I propose a scale starting at £1,000 and rising by annual increments of £50 to £1,200 - this to be supplemented by a lodging and subsistence allowance of £150 a year to meet the extra expenditure to which you refer in your letter.

In the case of Mr. Jenkins, the lodging allowance I suggest is £1 a week (this supplementing his pay of £7 a week).

Admiral Sir Lionel Halsey, ~~R.N.~~, G.C.M.G., G.C.V.O.,
K.C.I.E., C.B., ~~C———.~~,
St. James's Palace,
S.W.1.

Meanwhile, on 30 July 1936, Flight Lieutenant Fielden was promoted to the rank of wing commander in the Reserve of Air Force Officers. In addition to a salary of £1,000 per annum, he was entitled to a lodging and subsistence allowance of £150 per year. (*Queen's Flight Archive*)

Airspeed Envoy III G-AEXX was the first publicly funded Royal aircraft. It was delivered in the distinctive red and blue livery of the Brigade of Guards with silver cheat line and wings. It underwent flight testing at the A&AEE at Martlesham Heath in April and May 1937. (*Queen's Flight Archive A013*)

The cockpit of Airspeed Envoy III G-AEXX. (*Queen's Flight Archive*)

Once the Airspeed Envoy III had been delivered, it was soon put to work. It was busy on 9 May 1938 when the King once again visited a number of other RAF stations in connection with visits to factories busily engaged on meeting the increased orders placed for the RAF. He was photographed leaving Northolt in G-AEXX. (*Crown Copyright/Air Historical Branch image H490*)

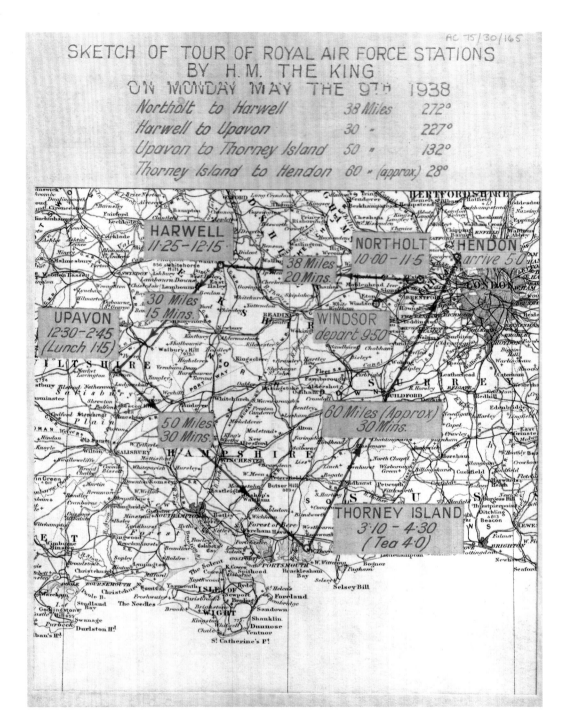

Map of a tour of RAF stations undertaken by the King on 9 May 1938. (*Queen's Flight Archives*)

BUCKINGHAM PALACE

8th. November, 1938.

My dear Newall,

I reported to The King our conversation the other day, and His Majesty approves of your various proposals for The King's Flight, and is grateful to you for the various measures which you are prepared to take with regard to it. The following arrangements will therefore hold good: -

(1)   The Flight will be stationed at Hendon, in new accommodation to be especially built for it away from the other hangars.

(2)   You will keep in touch with Fielden regarding the provision of a new machine. If the DH 95 proves to be satisfactory after its various trials, it may not be available before the end of next summer.

(3)   You will in due course make suggestions, after consultation with Fielden, regarding the appointment of an Assistant Pilot.

Copy of a letter from Buckingham Palace dated 8 November 1938 detailing various changes to be made to the ongoing operations of the King's Flight. The major change was the consideration of the de Havilland DH.95 Flamingo, which was later ordered. (*Queen's Flight Archive*)

(4)   The present personnel shall be retained (additions being made when necessary) until they are due for retirement, when it _may_ be considered more satisfactory to replace them from the Service. As regards qualifying for pensions, you will see what can be done about putting them on to the establishment, in the same way as other Civil employées of the Air Ministry.

I hope that this is a fair representation of the arrangement we provisionally made together, and which The King has now approved.

Yn- Sincerely,

A. H. L. Hawkins

Air Chief Marshal,
    Sir Cyril Newall, GCB., CMG., CBE.,
        Chief of the Air Staff,
    Air Ministry,
        Adastral House, Kingsway, W.C.2.

HRH King Edward VIII arriving at Harwell in G-AEXX during his tour of RAF stations on 9 May 1938. What appears to be a four-engine DH.86 is being marshalled from the right of the image. (*Queen's Flight Archives A536*)

In addition to the King, other members of the Royal Family were able to utilise the services of G-AEXX. In this photograph, the Duke and Duchess of Kent were photographed leaving the aircraft, although the date and location of the image were not noted. (*Queen's Flight Archive*)

The War Years 1939–45

When the Second World War seemed imminent, it was mooted that the King should have an aircraft with defensive armament, and the Lockheed Hudson was chosen. A Hudson 1, serial number N7263, arrived at Hendon for the King's Flight on 4 August 1939, direct from the Lockheed processing depot at Speke, near Liverpool. Work to convert it for royal use was immediately put in hand. (*Queen's Flight Archives*)

A Lockheed Hudson arrived at Hendon for the King's Flight on 4 August 1939, direct from the Lockheed processing depot at Speke, and work started immediately to convert the aircraft for Royal use. The aircraft was armed with two .303-inch Browning machine guns in a Boulton Paul turret and was camouflaged in the standard 'land scheme' of dark green and dark earth, although it carried no distinctive markings other than its military serial, N7283.

When war was declared on 3 September 1939, it was decided to move the King's Flight out of the London area and into RAF Benson, Oxfordshire. Here, Nos 52 and 63 Squadron arrived to act as training squadrons and were formed into No. 12 Operational Training Unit (OTU). The King's Flight became a lodger unit of the OTU.

Once the Hudson had arrived at Benson, the former Royal Envoy, G-AEXX, at last now wearing the military serial L7270 originally allocated in 1937, was sent to No. 24 (Communications) Squadron on 30 October 1939.

The Hudson was used by the King during the first year of the war but when the King visited the British Expeditionary Force (BEF) in France during December 1940, he went by sea with the RAF providing an air escort. One other aircraft joined the Flight on 15 March 1940, when Percival Q6 P5634 was delivered from its No. 24 (Communications) Squadron base at Northolt. This aircraft had been used by the AOC-in-C Bomber Command and was also occasionally used by the King.

Enter The de Havilland Flamingo

On 15 August, the King visited the de Havilland works at Hatfield and examined the next aircraft for the Flight – the DH.95 Flamingo.

The King's Flight now had three aircraft on strength – the Lockheed Hudson, Percival Q6 and the de Havilland Flamingo – and this was the peak strength achieved by the Flight during the war. Sadly, the Flamingo was the first to leave the Flight, when the King was concerned that the aircraft could better serve the war effort elsewhere. It followed the Airspeed Envoy to No. 24 (Communications) Squadron at Northolt on 14 February 1940 and its identity reverted to R2766. This move proved to be the first step in the wartime disbandment of the King's Flight.

During 1941, the aircraft of the King's Flight were rarely used and it was decided to disband the Flight as a separate unit. On 15 February 1942, it was officially absorbed into No. 161 Squadron, a special duties unit operating for the SOE, which formed at Newmarket that day from the nucleus of No. 138 Squadron personnel. Interestingly, Wing Commander E. H. Fielden was appointed to command the new squadron.

Gradually, the old personnel of the King's Flight at Benson were dispersed, while just a few remained until the remaining two aircraft were transferred. The Percival Q6 moved to Halton on 25 May 1942, while the former Royal Hudson moved to No. 161 Squadron on 22 June. According to records, the last individual to leave the Flight was G. O. Peskett, an Air Service assistant clerk who left on 29 June.

Avro York Ascalon

The wartime agreement that the British aircraft industry should concentrate on fighters and bombers, leaving the US manufacturers to supply the transport aircraft, was expedient at the time but later – in the immediate post-war years – proved to be somewhat unfortunate. However, one British-designed and manufactured transport aircraft did appear, despite the apparent moratorium. This was the Avro York and the third prototype – LV633 – was the first aircraft allotted to the RAF for delivery to No. 24 (Communications) Squadron at Hendon, as the personal transport for the Prime Minister, Winston Churchill. On 26 May 1943, the York, now named *Ascalon*, made its first trip, carrying Churchill to North Africa.

Once *Ascalon* had returned to Northolt, its captain was warned that it would be required again within the week. However, on this occasion, it was not to be Winston Churchill in the cabin. Initially, the crew speculated about the identity of their next passenger but all speculation ceased when Group Captain Fielden arrived at Northolt on 8 June and made a meticulous inspection of the Avro York.

At the flight briefing on 11 June, a message to the crew from Sir Frederick Bowhill, AOC-in-C of the newly formed Transport Command, put the official seal on the journey. Bowhill advised that the King was to visit his victorious troops in North Africa and it was to be the first occasion – either in times of peace or war – that a reigning monarch had left British shores by air, a duty previously conducted by the Royal Navy.

The crew were charged with His Majesty's safety. Radio silence was to be preserved throughout the trip. The plan was to fly *Ascalon* from the UK to North Africa via Gibraltar; flying well out to the west over the Atlantic to avoid any possible contact with German aircraft operating from occupied France. At pre-arranged turning points, warships of the Royal Navy were stationed and could be contacted by radio should the need arise. In the event of an engine failure or any other technical issue, the crew were to make for neutral Portugal.

The Royal party arrived at Northolt at 20:30 hours on 11 June, the King dressed in his Field Marshal's uniform for take-off at 23:00 hours. By the time Gibraltar air traffic control had informed the Moroccan authorities at Ras el Mer that the York was among many other UK aircraft being diverted that morning (*Ascalon*'s routine R/T call sign being one of those generally allotted), *Ascalon* was already in the circuit at Gibraltar.

Within an hour, *Ascalon* was on its way to Algiers and landed at Maison Blanche at 12:35 hours. After a visit to Supreme Headquarters and a tour of the British First Army troops, the Royal party flew on to Oran (La Senia) on 14 June to review elements of the US Fifth Army. Later, on 17 June, the King flew to Tunis to see more of the Allied forces. On 19 June, *Ascalon* continued eastwards with the Royal party to Tripoli, where a reception was held for them. The King and his party embarked on a short visit to Malta aboard HMS *Aurora* before returning on 21 June.

The return flight left Tripoli on 22 June, and Algiers on 24 June. The York landed at Northolt one hour ahead of schedule, but both the CAS and the AOC-in-C, Transport Command, along with the station commander of RAF Northolt, were on hand to greet the King. The trip had been the longest Royal flight of all time, but it was to be surpassed in distance the following year.

The second Royal flight in *Ascalon* was on similar lines to the first. Once again, the York had returned from a trip to North Africa when its crew were alerted to the next VIP flight, especially when Group Captain Fielden provided the liaison. On this occasion, the King intended visiting his troops in Italy and the only route offering any degree of safety was via North Africa.

During the evening of 22 July 1944, the King arrived at RAF Northolt for his journey. On hand to see him off were the Queen and Princess Elizabeth. As they climbed aboard to say their farewells, a V1 flying bomb was heard, and then seen, approaching from the south-east. With the nearest air raid shelter some considerable distance from the aircraft, there was little the crew could do except watch the flight of the 'Doodlebug', which passed over Northolt and wreaked its havoc elsewhere in London. The aircraft eventually departed Northolt at 23:10 hours.

The King visited the Anzio beach-head; saw British, American, Polish and Brazilian forces; held investitures; watched artillery duels; and visited the United States Navy flagship offshore. The King left Naples for home on 2 August, once again staging through Rabat-Salé before arriving back at Northolt on 3 August. As the aircraft touched down at 07:15 hours, the King was reminded that V1 activity was still a significant menace when another one passed over Northolt as their aircraft taxied back to the ramp.

A Change of Organisation for Royal Flights

The responsibility for the Royal flights was now taken over by the Metropolitan Communications Squadron, which formed at Hendon in April 1944 following the re-naming of No. 510 Squadron. It was equipped with thirty Percival Proctors, along with various quantities of DH.89 Dominies, Lockheed 12As, Hudsons (two of which were specially equipped as ambulance aircraft), Airspeed Oxfords, V-S Spitfires, Avro Ansons, Miles Messengers, Percival Q6s and Dakotas; all were based at Hendon. The Metropolitan Communications Squadron also operated three Avro York I aircraft – including *Ascalon* – which were based at Northolt.

Despite the best-laid plans of the Metropolitan Communications Squadron at Hendon to fly the King in one of the squadron aircraft, it appears he may have had other ideas! He had been impressed with General Sir Henry Maitland Wilson's Dakota in Italy and in view of the excellent safety record of the type, it was decided to allot one to No. 24 Squadron for future Royal flights. As a consequence of this action, No. 24 Squadron could then continue in their traditional role of arranging such flights. On the other hand, it was a definite break from tradition that a British monarch should be flown regularly in an aircraft not made in Britain.

Dakota IV KN386 was selected for the King. The aircraft had been provided under the Lease/ Lend allocation and was delivered to the UK on 4 March 1945. A week later it was sent to No. 5 MU at Kemble for fitting out. However, before its arrival into service, the war in Europe came to an end on 8 May 1945 and the event was celebrated with parties all over the UK.

Once KN386 had been completed, it was allotted to No. 24 Squadron at Hendon and on the evening of 6 June was flown to Northolt to fly the King and Queen to the Channel Islands the following morning. Leaving Northolt at 09:45 hours, the Dakota touched down on the liberated soil of Jersey just 100 minutes later. The Royal party joined the aircraft again at 15:00 hours for the twenty-minute flight to Guernsey, before returning to Northolt at 18:25 hours.

After the peak period of the summer of 1945, the King had little occasion to fly for many months and KN386 became a general VIP aircraft. Once again, no specific aircraft were allotted for the King and suggestions were being made that a King's Flight should again be constituted.

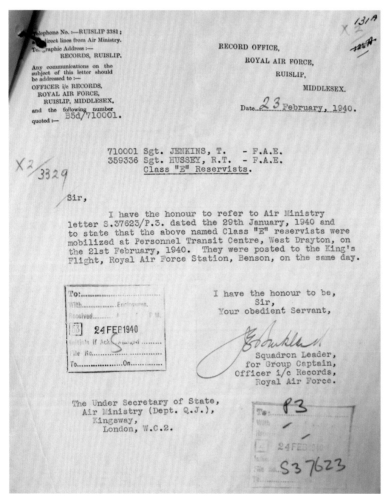

Official paperwork from the Records Office of the Royal Air Force in February 1940, confirming that former reservist sergeants Jenkins and Hussey were both formally mobilised into service with the King's Flight, now stationed at Benson. (*Queen's Flight Archives*)

An order had been placed with de Havilland for one of their new DH.95 Flamingo aircraft. This image of the aircraft – registered as G-AGCC – was thought to be taken at Hatfield on 6 August 1940. (*BAE Systems image 17904*)

An image of the DH.95 Flamingo interior, taken ahead of the aircraft entering service with the King's Flight. (*Queen's Flight Archives*)

A Percival P.16e Petrel, also known as the Q6 – P5634 – was allocated to the King's Flight on 15 March 1940 for light liaison duties. It was subsequently used by C-in-C Bomber Command and was re-allocated to RAF Halton on 25 May 1942. (*Queen's Flight Archives*)

On 15 August 1940, the King visited the de Havilland factory at Hatfield to inspect the new DH.95 Flamingo. When at the site, he took a tour of the facilities accompanied by Geoffrey de Havilland. (*BAE Systems*)

The King was photographed stepping from the DH.95 Flamingo after having been shown around the aircraft by Geoffrey de Havilland on 15 August 1940. G-AGCC was fitted out to deluxe standards, with two cabins and repositioned windows. There were so few in service, however, that the King became concerned that its operations might be placing a strain upon support resources and by 14 February 1942 it had been passed to No. 24 Squadron. (Queen's Flight Archives)

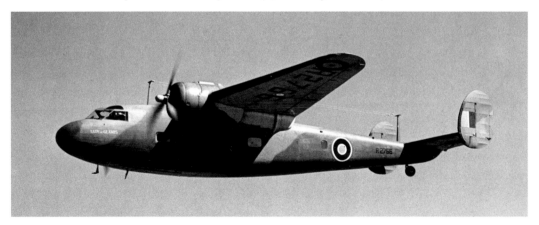

The identity of the Flamingo, as with the earlier Envoy, was a matter of some controversy. The RAF serial R2766 was officially allocated but after the fall of France, and with the Battle of Britain raging ahead of a presumed invasion, it was considered expedient to have the aircraft registered as a civil aircraft to facilitate passage through neutral countries in the event of an emergency. It reverted to its civilian registration, G-AGCC, but continued to carry its RAF roundels. (*Crown Copyright/Air Historical Branch image CH5853*)

The King was a regular visitor to RAF stations throughout the Second World War. He was photographed while inspecting Hawker Typhoon 1B MN454 at RAF Northolt in 1943. (*BAE Systems*)

An image of Wing Commander Edward Fielden, probably taken around the time he was commanding No. 161 Squadron, the unit that had officially absorbed the King's Flight following its disbandment on 14 February 1942. (*Queen's Flight Archives*)

In November 1943, King George VI and Queen Elizabeth visited RAF Tempsford, where Group Captain Edward Fielden was station commander, having been appointed to the role on 1 October 1942. The Lysander in the background is probably a Mk IIIA example from the resident No. 161 Squadron. (*Queen's Flight Archives image A046*)

Avro York C.I LV633 *Ascalon* was a VVIP standard aircraft operated by No. 24 Squadron at Hendon and was primarily used by Prime Minister Winston Churchill. The aircraft was photographed on 2 June 1943, taking off from Chateaudun, Algeria, with Winston Churchill and Anthony Eden on board. On 11 June 1943, the aircraft was used by King George VI to visit his victorious troops in North Africa – a trip that routed via Gibraltar and Algiers. The aircraft returned to the UK on 25 June. (*Crown Copyright/Air Historical Branch image CNA4152*)

Standing out from its contemporaries on the ramp at Prague in 1945 is VVIP Dakota IV KN386, used by the Royal Family and one of a number of the type operated by No. 24 Squadron. KN386 was operated in a highly polished natural metal finish. (*Queen's Flight Archives image A588*)

Another No. 24 Squadron VVIP aircraft used was Dakota III KG770. It was photographed in flight in June 1945 with King George VI and Queen Elizabeth on board while returning from a visit to the Channel Islands in June 1945. (*Crown Copyright/Air Historical Branch image CH15397*)

The King's Flight is Re-formed
1946–53

A spectacular air-to-air study of Vickers Viking C(VVIP).2 VL246 taken just ahead of the aircraft's entry into service with the King's Flight at Benson in 1947. (*Queen's Flight Archive*)

Following the end of the Second World War, it quickly became apparent that Royal travel by air, especially over long distances, would become the norm. Following representations to the King, he gave formal approval to the reconstitution of the King's Flight and confirmed the appointment of Air Commodore E. H. Fielden, CB, CVO, DFC, AFC, as Captain of the Flight.

Early in 1946, the question of aircraft type and the numbers required for the Flight was discussed; there was firm agreement on the Vickers VC1. This aircraft had originated from a Vickers submission to the Brabazon Committee in 1944 as an interim transport based on the Wellington bomber with some of the refinements used in the Warwick, while introducing a stressed-skin fuselage. The VC1 prototype had made its maiden flight from Wisley on 22 June 1945 and was the first British post-war civil transport to fly. It was also the first post-war aircraft to comply with the new ICAO regulations for take-off with asymmetric power. The VC1 was soon named the Viking and on 5 April 1946, the Ministry of Aircraft Production placed an order for fifty; on 24 April, the type was granted its Certificate of Airworthiness.

On 1 May 1946, authority was given for the establishment of the King's Flight at RAF Benson, the base having been transferred from Coastal Command to Transport Command. Initially, the flight establishment consisted of one Avro York for VVIP work; two Vickers Viking aircraft for VVIP work; plus another two Viking aircraft for normal passenger use. In August this complement was changed to a pair of Viking C(VVIP).2 aircraft, with another C.2 as a freighter and a fourth C.2 configured as a mobile workshop.

Selection of Personnel

The selection of personnel for the King's Flight had been ongoing throughout 1946. For his deputy, Fielden chose Wing Commander E. W. Tacon, DSO, DFC, AFC, a New Zealander who had been taken a prisoner of war in 1944 towards the end of his third tour of operations.

Soon after his appointment, Tacon took a Viking, flown by some of the recently selected aircrew, to South Africa, ahead of the forthcoming Royal tour, to visit the various airfields the Royal party would be expected to fly in and out of.

The first Viking to arrive with the Flight was C.2 VL245, which landed at Benson on 12 August 1946. This was the Royal staff aircraft and had required the least number of modifications from standard. The remaining three Vikings arrived at Benson in January 1947 with C(VVIP).2 VL246 being allocated for the King, and C(VVIP).2 VL247 for the Queen, along with the special workshop aircraft C.2, VL248.

Tour of Africa

The King and Queen, accompanied by the two princesses, Elizabeth and Margaret, set out from Portsmouth on 1 February 1947 aboard the Royal Navy's newest battleship, HMS *Vanguard*, which Princess Elizabeth had named at its launching ceremony a little over three years earlier. The Vikings had left earlier, flying separately to Brooklyn Air Station, near Cape Town, which was their base for the tour.

Taking the Royal Family to various parts of South Africa, Northern Rhodesia and Southern Rhodesia, the Vikings flew around 160,000 miles without incident. Interestingly, shortly after the Royal visit, South African Airways placed an order for eight Vikings. The Royal Family returned to Britain aboard HMS *Vanguard* during April.

During the next few years, the VVIP Vikings were used regularly for Royal visits. One mishap did occur, however, while the Royal Family were at Balmoral. A daily Viking flight from London to Dyce Airport, near Aberdeen, brought official mail. Upon returning one day in September, the staff aircraft – VL245 – developed mechanical problems shortly after take-off from Dyce. Subsequently, a forced landing was made in a field but the aircraft ran into a stone wall and was badly damaged. An RAF Viking was lent to the Flight while the aircraft was recovered and repairs could be completed.

King's Flight Begins Rotary Operations

In 1947, the King's Flight had its first experience of operating a helicopter. In order to deliver mail from Dyce, the nearest airfield to Balmoral, a Sikorsky R-4 Hoverfly helicopter was used in a shuttle service from Dyce to a cricket pitch in the grounds of Balmoral Castle.

Following the Royal visit to South Africa in early 1947, the most extensive period of flying for the King's Flight Viking aircraft was in November. The aircraft conveyed Royal guests from and to the Continent for the wedding of Princess Elizabeth and Philip Mountbatten at Westminster Abbey on 20 November. On the morning of the wedding, Philip was made the Duke of Edinburgh.

Another Commonwealth visit for the King and Queen was planned for the end of 1948 – this time to Australia and New Zealand. The plans were modelled on those of the previous South Africa tour. The Royal Family would sail in a battleship but air travel was essential to cover the vast distances involved in the territories to be visited. Fielden and Tacon, along with two other officers and five airmen, flew to Australia and New Zealand to survey all of the airfields that would be used.

Experience from the South Africa tour had found that, in an ideal situation, five and not four Vikings were required for such trips. This would allow for one staff Viking to leave before the

Royal party with attendants, police and luggage. Twenty minutes later, the King's Viking would leave, followed in five minutes by the Queen's aircraft. Finally, the maintenance (workshop) aircraft would follow twenty-five minutes later, leaving one Viking on standby in case any of the other aircraft should go unserviceable.

The original staff aircraft, VL245, which had suffered a mishap in 1947 (see above), was replaced in July 1948 by two RAF Viking C.2 aircraft – VL232 and VL233. These two, along with VL246, VL247 and VL248, completed the fleet of the King's Flight and were scheduled to leave for Australia on 29 November. Shortly before the first Viking was due to leave, it was announced by the Palace that the visit was cancelled on the advice of the King's doctors.

Subsequently, the Viking aircraft were rarely used by the King and Queen, although many other flights were undertaken for official visits by other members of the Royal Family. Princess Elizabeth was a regular passenger, taking a number of trips to Malta.

BOAC Stratocruiser

The deteriorating health of the King did not permit another Commonwealth Tour and the invitations were passed to Princess Elizabeth and her consort; visits to Canada, Australia and New Zealand were planned. However, the Vikings with their 6.5-hour endurance at a mere 200 mph cruising speed were not in the transatlantic class. Consequently, it was arranged for the Royal couple to fly to Canada by BOAC (British Overseas Airways Corporation) in the Boeing 377 Stratocruiser *Canopus*.

This was the first time that a member of the Royal Family had crossed the Atlantic by air and it provided a great boost to transatlantic air travel. *Canopus* departed at 00:15 hours on 8 October 1951. Avro Shackleton MR.1s, which had only entered RAF service earlier that year, provided escort patrols for the first 1,300 miles out from the UK, from where Royal Canadian Air Force (RCAF) maritime reconnaissance aircraft took over. In addition, five Royal Navy warships were stationed along the route at 300-mile intervals. The journey was uneventful.

During the visit, the Royal couple were conveyed in an RCAF Canadair C-4 Argonaut, a modified Canadian-built Douglas C-54 Skymaster powered by four Rolls-Royce Merlin engines.

To meet further invitations from East African territories, it was decided to visit East Africa as a step on the way to the Australasia visit. This time it was a BOAC Argonaut, *Atlanta*, that carried Princess Elizabeth and the Duke of Edinburgh. The Argonaut left London Airport for Nairobi at noon on 31 January 1952 and flew to El Adam, Libya, where a new BOAC crew took over. For local flying in East Africa, an East African Airways Dakota RMA *Sagana* was used.

On 6 February 1953, the King died while the Royal couple were still in East Africa. The following day, the Princess and her husband flew back to England in an Argonaut.

Following a lengthy period of mourning, the new Queen was crowned at Westminster Abbey on 2 June 1953. The coronation of the Queen was the first ever to be televised (although the BBC Television Service had covered part of the procession from Westminster Abbey after her father's coronation in 1937), and was also the world's first major international event to be broadcast on television.

It was also announced that Her Majesty would accept the appointments formerly held by her father of Air Commodore-in-Chief to the Royal Auxiliary Air Force, Royal Air Force Regiment and the Royal Observer Corps. In the case of Air Commodore-in-Chief to the Air Training Corps, the late King was succeeded by the Duke of Edinburgh. At the same time the Royal Flight became officially known as the Queen's Flight and Air Commodore Fielden was confirmed in his appointment as its Captain.

The King's Flight Airspeed Consul III, G-AEXX, had been impressed into RAF service in 1939 as L7270, where it operated with No. 24 (Communications) Squadron from 30 October. After the war it reverted to its civilian identity of G-AEXX on its sale to an owner at Hanworth aerodrome in February 1946. It was later sold to an owner in Sweden, who registered the aircraft as SE-ASN. (*Queen's Flight Archives A226*)

Vickers Viking C(VVIP).2 VL245, the Royal staff aircraft of the King's Flight, was the first of the type delivered, on 12 August 1946. It was photographed on the grass at Wisley in October of the same year. (*Crown Copyright/Air Historical Branch image R339*)

A nice air-to-air study of the King's personal Viking C(VVIP).2, VL246. After extensive modifications for its VVIP role, it was delivered to the Flight in early 1947. At the time of the photographs, the code '1' had not yet been added to the tail fin and fuselage of the aircraft. (*Queen's Flight Archive*)

The Royal saloon onboard Viking C(VVIP).2 VL246. (*Queen's Flight Archive*)

Viking C(VVIP).2 VL247 was allocated as the personal aircraft of Her Majesty the Queen. Later, it had the number '2' added to the tail fin and under the nose. It was photographed while taxiing at London Airport with a member of the Royal Family aboard, hence the Royal emblem being flown. (*BAE Systems*)

The fourth Viking aircraft in the King's Flight fleet was a C.2 variant, VL248. The aircraft, which joined the Flight in January 1947, was fitted out with workshop and maintenance equipment for the other VIP-equipped Vikings of the King's Flight. (*Crown Copyright/Air Historical Branch image PRB-1-829*)

The fuselage interior of 'flying workshop' VL248, which was well equipped for its task. (*Queen's Flight Archives*)

The cockpit of Viking C(VVIP).2 VL246, taken at the Vickers factory just before delivery to the King's Flight at Benson in 1947. (*Vickers (Aircraft) Limited via Queen's Flight Archive*)

The instrument panel and engine control levers in the cockpit of Viking C(VVIP).2 VL246. (*Vickers (Aircraft) Limited via Queen's Flight Archive*)

Africa Tour 1947

It didn't take long for all four Vikings to be called in action. By February 1947, all four aircraft had established themselves on the Brooklyn Air Base near Cape Town, ahead of the Royal tour to South Africa. The Queen and Princess Elizabeth were photographed leaving the King's aircraft, VL246, during the tour. (*Queen's Flight Archive*)

HRH Princess Margaret at the bottom of the steps of Viking VL246 just after arriving at Bloemfontein. The King and Queen travelled with princesses Elizabeth and Margaret on the Royal tour. (*BAE Systems*)

The Royal party at Bloemfontein. King George VI was photographed with the flight crew of Viking C(VVIP).2 VL246. (*Queen's Flight Archive*)

All four of the King's Flight Vikings parked on the ramp at Bloemfontein. The King's personal aircraft, VL246, nearest the camera, was using the call sign 'Evening Star'. (*Queen's Flight Archive*)

An unofficial but rare colour image from the 1947 Royal tour to South Africa showing both the flight and ground crew of the King's personal Viking, VL246. Left to right are: Flt Lt Reid (Radio Officer); Flt Lt Fowkes (Navigator); Flt Lt Lee (2nd Pilot); Wg Comm Tacon (CO and Pilot); Cpl Reynolds (Engines); Cpl Bulled (Airframe); and LAC Elliot (Steward). (*Queen's Flight Archive A846*)

Sadly, Viking VL245 came to grief on 12 September 1947. At the time, the Royal Family was in residence at Balmoral and the aircraft was undertaking the daily official mail delivery. Shortly after take-off from Aberdeen while en route to Benson, VL245 developed engine problems with a runaway propeller and made a forced landing in a field, demolishing a stone wall in the process. The aircraft was substantially damaged and never returned to the King's Flight. (*Queen's Flight Archive*)

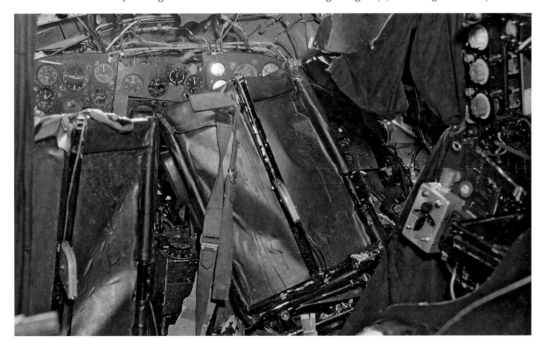

A photograph that clearly demonstrates the extensive damage to the cockpit area on VL245. (*Queen's Flight Archive*)

King George VI photographed leaving his personal Viking C(VVIP).2, VL246, during an official engagement. Queen Elizabeth can be seen just leaving the cabin. (*Queen's Flight Archive*)

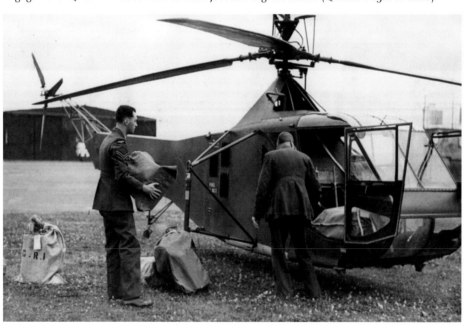

Mail deliveries during the summer of 1947 provided the King's Flight with its first experience of helicopter operations. Two Hoverfly Mk 1 helicopters were borrowed from the Royal Navy in August and flown to Dyce Airport, Aberdeen, from where they were able to shuttle the mail to and from the cricket pitch at Balmoral. (*Queen's Flight Archive A580*)

One of the Hoverfly Mk 1 helicopters photographed en route to Balmoral for the daily mail shuttle. (*Queen's Flight Archive A595*)

Flight Lieutenants A. J. Lee and E. B. Trubshaw (*right*), the King's Flight's first two helicopter pilots, trained *ab initio* for the task, seen conversing in front of one of the Flight's two Hoverfly helicopters. (*Queen's Flight Archive A066*)

Princess Elizabeth and Prince Philip
in conversation with Air Commodore
Edward Fielden at Benson in 1949 as
Philip was about to leave for Malta.
(*Queen's Flight Archive*)

In 1949, the Queen Mother used the services of a BOAC Comet 1 for a Royal tour. (*Queen's Flight Archive A083*)

HRH Princess Margaret visited Hatfield during the National Air Races in 1951 and was photographed in the Comet 1 cockpit with Sir Geoffrey de Havilland and John Cunningham. Later, she requested an opportunity to fly in the new Comet. (*Queen's Flight Archive A085b*)

On 31 January 1952, Princess Elizabeth and the Duke of Edinburgh flew out of London Airport on *Atlanta*, a BOAC Canadair C.4 Argonaut, G-ALHK, to begin a tour of East Africa. While the Royal party were in East Africa, the King died. The Argonaut conveyed their Royal Highnesses from Entebbe to London on 7 February, where they were met by Winston Churchill and Clement Attlee. (*Queen's Flight Archive*)

In May 1952, Prince Philip decided to learn to fly, and felt the only way to learn properly was to be taught by the RAF. Two Chipmunks were allocated to the Flight for the duration of the training: WP961 and WP912. His instructor was Flt Lt Caryl Gordon. Philip made his first solo flight on 20 December 1952. (*Crown Copyright/Air Historical Branch PRB-1-17949*)

From: Group Captain Peter Townsend, C.V.O., D.S.O., D.F.C.

Confidential.

BUCKINGHAM PALACE

8th April, 1952.

Dear Sir Geoffrey,

Queen Elizabeth, the Queen Mother, wishes me to write and say how much both Her Majesty and Princess Margaret would like to go for a flight in a Comet. You will remember, I expect, that Her Royal Highness expressed a wish to do so when she visited Hatfield last Summer.

Her Majesty would wish her visit to Hatfield and the subsequent flight to be quite private and informal, and if it can be conveniently arranged, she would like to come over from Windsor on a fine day during the week beginning 14th April, or the following week.

I shall be at Buckingham Palace until noon on Thursday, 10th April: thereafter at Windsor Castle. I could call at Hatfield on my way to Windsor on Thursday - otherwise perhaps one of your staff could come and discuss the details with me here or at Windsor.

Yours sincerely,

Peter Townsend.

Captain Sir Geoffrey de Havilland, C.B.E.

A letter from Buckingham Palace to Sir Geoffrey de Havilland in April 1952 requesting a flight in the new Comet jet airliner for HM the Queen Mother and Princess Margaret. (*Queen's Flight Archive*)

26ᵗ May 1952

BUCKINGHAM PALACE

Dear Sir Geoffrey. Queen Elizabeth wishes me to write and thank you for all the trouble you took to arrange such a perfect flight in the Comet last Friday.

Her Majesty and Princess Margaret thought the aeroplane was so beautiful and the passengers and crew so nice to them; and favoured as we were by such a lovely day, they enjoyed the flight beyond all measure.

They were so pleased, too, to have the chance of going round the workshops and meeting some of those responsible for the Comet's excellence of design and construction.

Queen Elizabeth and Princess Margaret wish me to say how deeply grateful they are to you for such a wonderful and uplifting experience and how very touched they were by your kindness in inviting them.

Yours sincerely.

Peter Townsend.

P.S. May I add my own special thanks. I am so grateful to you for the flight, which was perfect in every way.

After making a trip in the aircraft at Hatfield, the Queen Mother wrote to Sir Geoffrey de Havilland in May 1952, expressing her gratitude for the 'perfect flight'. (*Queen's Flight Archive*)

59

HRH the Duke of Edinburgh sitting in the cockpit of a Comet jet airliner during his visit to the de Havilland factory at Hatfield in March 1952. Prince Philip made a flight in Comet 1 G-ALYP during his visit, accompanied by John Cunningham and Peter Bois. (*Queen's Flight Archive A085a*)

In January 1953, the Duke of Edinburgh made one of his regular visits to Malta, this time utilising a British European Airways (BEA) Airspeed AS.57 Ambassador, G-AMAB, *Sir Francis Bacon*. This represented BEA's first Royal flight. For his arrival at Valetta, the Royal ensign was carried above the cockpit. (*BAE Systems*)

The Queen's Flight 1953–68

The Queen Mother and Princess Margaret arrive back at London Airport on 30 June 1953 after a flight aboard a BOAC Comet 1, G-ALYW, after a Royal visit to Rhodesia. (*de Havilland Aircraft Company negative DH7171A via BAE Systems*)

Following the Coronation of Her Majesty Queen Elizabeth II at Westminster Abbey on 2 June 1953, the following years saw many changes to the Queen's Flight.

Despite having only flown around 800 hours with the Flight, the workshop Viking C.2, VL248, was withdrawn from use in 1953. This amount of hours was not considered excessive by any means, as British European Airways (BEA) were averaging nearer to 8,000 hours on each of their Viking airframes. VL248 was sold to Mexican Air Lines.

The following year a Sikorsky Dragonfly HC.4 helicopter was added to the Flight. Up until this point, helicopters had only carried mail for the Royal Flight, but it was now envisaged that they would be used for passenger carrying.

de Havilland Heron Joins The Flight

The Duke of Edinburgh had been undergoing flying training and by the middle of 1953 had been flying Devon VP961, which had been temporarily attached to the Queen's Flight. Then, in May 1955, a de Havilland DH.114 Heron C.3 joined the Flight, representing the first stage of its re-equipment, which, for the previous nine years, had consisted entirely of Viking aircraft. XH375 was handed over by Sir Geoffrey de Havilland at Hatfield on 18 May and was designated Prince Philip's personal aircraft. By September the name 'Duke of Edinburgh' was appearing in the Operational Record Book crew listing for the Heron C.3 as frequently as in the passenger listing.

In 1955, Prince Philip also qualified as a helicopter pilot after training under Lieutenant-Commander M. H. Simpson, the CFI of No. 705 Squadron, Royal Navy, at Gosport. Initially, a Westland WS-51 Dragonfly HR.1 was used and based at White Waltham. Later, a Westland Whirlwind from No. 705 Squadron was used for official visits and was later also being flown by the Duke. Shortly afterwards, the Queen Mother and Princess Margaret, along with the Duke and Duchess of Gloucester, were regularly using helicopters for their official visits.

On 2 November 1956, the Queen made a formal inspection of her Flight, which now numbered eighty officers and men. At the time, the Duke was on a Royal visit to the other side of the world, which had involved a variety of aircraft. He had flown from London Airport in a BOAC Canadair Argonaut, G-ALHD *Ajax*, to Mombasa, where he joined the Royal yacht en route to Australia, where he opened the Olympic Games in Melbourne. Having staged in Malaya, the Duke flew from Butterworth to the recently expanded airfield at Kuala Lumpur in a highly polished Hastings of the Far East Transport Wing. While in Australia and New Zealand, the Duke was flown in a variety of aircraft, including a Convair 440 and Dakotas of both the RAAF and RAN.

Vikings Out With New Herons and helicopters In

1958 was certainly a year of change for the Queen's Flight. The remaining three Viking aircraft were withdrawn from service and were eventually sold to Tradair. They were replaced by a pair of new de Havilland Heron C.4 aircraft with the serial numbers XM295 and XM296. During the year, the first specification was issued for the fitting-out of helicopters to a VVIP standard suitable for use with the Queen's Flight. The initial plan had been to modify a pair of Westland Whirlwind HAS.7 airframes for this purpose and as an interim measure the single Dragonfly was replaced by a Whirlwind HAR.4 XL111.

V-bomber Flight

On 24 June 1958, the Duke took a flight aboard Victor B.1 XA900 from RAF Wyton. The aircraft was commanded by Wing Commander F. Dodd, OC of No. 230 OCU. A maximum rate climb was made to 40,000 feet before the aircraft levelled and cruised at 600 knots. Next it flew a simulated nuclear attack on the town of Andover, before completing a demonstrated radar controlled approach to, and before landing, at Farnborough.

RAF Versus Commercial Airlines

Around this time, there was much criticism in the media that the RAF's Comet 2C aircraft of No. 216 Squadron – the world's first pure jet passenger aircraft – were not being used for the 1957 Royal visit to Canada and the United States. The de Havilland Comet was in need of a boost, having recently suffered unfortunate accidents to some of the older versions of the aircraft.

For every overseas Royal visit since the war, the use of either civilian or military aircraft for the task has been carefully considered. With the Comet 2C, it was well within the Royal Air Force's capability to convey the Royal Family anywhere in the world, irrespective of the limitations of the aircraft then in use with the Queen's Flight. The use by the Royal Family of British civil airline aircraft was very much in the interest of the British airlines – particularly if operating British-manufactured types.

When British European Airways (BEA) introduced the Airspeed Ambassador into regular service back in 1952, BEA arranged their first Royal flight in the same year by taking the Duke of Edinburgh in G-AMAB, named *Francis Bacon*, to Malta. In January 1953, when BEA received the first Vickers Viscount into service, they arranged to take Princess Margaret from London to Oslo in G-AMOB, named *RMA William Baffin*. On a Royal visit to Canada in 1957, the Queen and the Duke crossed the Atlantic in a BOAC Douglas DC-7C, an aircraft BOAC had only just introduced into service.

Both the Queen and Prince Philip had already flown in a Comet 2C. On 4 June 1957, while the Royal Family were in residence at Sandringham, they flew from RAF Marham in a No. 216 Squadron aircraft before landing at RAF Leuchars just fifty-five minutes later. Later, in 1959, the Duke flew to India and Pakistan in a BOAC Comet 4 and later joined the Queen on an Atlantic crossing aboard another BOAC Comet. Meanwhile, the Queen Mother and Princess Margaret had flown to Rome in a No. 216 Squadron Comet C.2.

During this period, the Herons made a number of major tours, including a visit by the Duke and Duchess of Gloucester to Ethiopia, British Somaliland and Aden in late 1958, and to Nigeria in 1959. Also in 1959, Prince Philip flew to India, Pakistan, Sarawak and Brunei at the beginning of the year and to West Africa towards the end of the year, while the Queen Mother visited Kenya and Uganda.

Whirlwind HCC.8s Arrive

By the end of the 1950s, the Herons were the mainstay of the Queen's Flight, although Devon VP961 was also used occasionally. In November 1959, the first VVIP helicopters arrived on the Flight, when Whirlwind HCC.8s XN126 and XN127 were delivered.

Into the 1960s with Dayglo Paint

The early 1960s represented a period when red and orange Dayglo paint patches were appearing on both military and civilian aircraft as a flight safety measure to improve an aircraft's conspicuousness. Although it would ruin the immaculate appearance of the aircraft of the Queen's Flight, already resplendent in blue and red trimming on a highly polished natural metal surface, the decision was taken to paint all of the aircraft an overall fluorescent red. This new high-visibility red colour scheme was completed by the end of 1961.

By this time, the first 'airmiss' of a sovereign aircraft had been reported; although the aircraft involved was painted in Transport Command's standard white and grey colour scheme, not the new 'royal red'. The 'airmiss' occurred on 25 October 1960, when the Queen and the Duke of Edinburgh were returning from Denmark in a No. 216 Squadron Comet C.2, XK696 *Orion*. When XK696 was around 20 miles north-east of Eelde (near Groningen, Holland), at 35,000 feet, the co-pilot of the Comet spotted two aircraft on a collision course. They were identified as F-86 Sabres of the Luftwaffe, both of which banked away immediately following the sighting. An Anglo-German commission of inquiry was set-up to investigate the incident. The Sabre pilots reported that they had the Comet in view and that there had been no danger of collision. As there were conflicting reports of the proximity of the fighters, a definite conclusion could not be reached and the matter was closed.

For the Asian tour of 1961, the Queen flew out in an RAF Britannia aircraft, although for local flying the venerable Dakota was once again called upon to operate in the mountainous regions of Nepal. The Heron aircraft of the Queen's Flight lacked both load-carrying capacity and performance. Two Dakota aircraft were used; KN645, which had once been the personal transport of Field Marshal Lord Montgomery, and KN452, which had recently returned from Malta, where it had been in use with the AOC for special flights.

More Changes to the Flight

On 6 May 1964, the first of the Gnome-powered Whirlwind helicopters arrived. This change reflected the general service changeover to the Whirlwind HAR.10, with the VVIP models for the Queen's Flight being designated HCC.12. Two Whirlwind HCC.12s replaced the earlier HCC.8 variants during the spring.

Then, on 9 July, the first Hawker Siddeley Andover CC.2 – XS789 – arrived at Benson. The Duke had already been flying the civil demonstrator and was familiar with the type. The second Andover CC.2 – XS790 – arrived on 7 August.

The Andover CC.2s were from a batch of six VVIP aircraft ordered, with the remaining four aircraft serving with RAF Middle East and RAF Far East Communications Flights, No. 32 Squadron at Northolt and No. 21 Squadron in Germany. The two aircraft for the Queen's Flight were fitted out with an executive suite and forward cabin, although the Royal Andover CC.2 aircraft were designed to be convertible to regular transport aircraft in an emergency. Normal crew of four consisted of pilot, co-pilot, supernumerary and cabin attendant.

The first Royal flight in a VC10 was on 1 February 1965, when the Queen made her state visit to Ethiopia in BOAC VC.10 G-ARVL. The 3,750-mile flight from London Airport to Addis Ababa was flown non-stop in just 7 hours. Later that month, when the Duke and Duchess of Kent flew to Gambia for the Independence celebrations, Britannia C.2 XN404 *Canopus* from No. 511 Squadron was used.

A New Captain Ends in Tragedy

On 1 August 1964, Air Commodore J. H. L. Blount, DFC, had taken over as Captain of the Queen's Flight. However, his tenure was relatively short-lived as, on 7 December 1967, he was flying in Whirlwind HCC.12 XR487 when it crashed. It marked the first serious accident in the history of the Flight, dating back to 1936. While flying from Benson to the Westland facility at Yeovil, the rotor shaft snapped as the Whirlwind was flying at 500 feet over the Berkshire village of Brightwalton. All of the crew, including Air Commodore Blunt, perished in the accident.

A standard Whirlwind HAR.10, XP299, was used as a temporary replacement for the crashed HCC.12 and in February 1968 Air Commodore A. L. Winskill, CBE, DFC and Bar, was appointed as the new Captain of the Queen's Flight.

Farewell to the Heron

In June 1968, the last of the Heron aircraft were withdrawn from service in the Queen's Flight. They had served the Flight well, having made 941 Royal flights, covering 13,400 hours and around 2 million miles between them. Their periods of service with the Flight were as follows:

XH375	May 1955 to September 1964	3,560 flying hours
XM295	April 1958 to January 1965	3,710 flying hours
XM296	April 1958 to July 1968	4,310 flying hours
XR391	June 1961 to June 1968	1,820 flying hours

State Visit to South America in VC.10 C.1

For the Queen's state visit to South America at the end of 1968, VC.10 C.1 XV107 of No. 10 Squadron, RAF Support Command, was specially equipped and was supported by a Comet from No. 216 Squadron along with one of the Queen's Flight Andover CC.2 aircraft.

The Duke of Edinburgh had been steadily pursuing a course of flying instruction, and in mid-1953 had been flying Devon C.1 VP961, which had been temporarily attached to the Queen's Flight. (*Queen's Flight Archive*)

The Queen and Prince Philip visited New Zealand in January 1954. During their visit, they flew from Rotorua to Gisborne in a de Havilland Heron 1 of the New Zealand National Airways Corporation. (*Queen's Flight Archive A088a*)

HM the Queen Mother leaving Westland Dragonfly HC.4 XF261, which had been on loan to the Queen's Flight between September 1954 and August 1958 from the Central Flying School. (*Crown Copyright/RAF Benson via Queen's Flight Archive A824*)

The handover of the Duke of Edinburgh's Heron C.3, XH375, by Sir Geoffrey de Havilland at Hatfield on 18 March 1955. (*de Havilland Aircraft Company image DH8658M via BAE Systems*)

Heron C.3 XH375 parked outside the flight shed at Hatfield on 18 March 1955, just ahead of the formal delivery of the aircraft to the Duke of Edinburgh. (*de Havilland Aircraft Company via BAE Systems*)

Despite having already taken delivery of the new Heron C.3 XH375, the Queen and Prince Philip used Viking C(VVIP).2 VL246 for their visit to RAF Moreton Valence on 3 May 1955. (*Queen's Flight Archive*)

The new Heron C.3 was soon popular with members of the Royal Family. Between 28 January and 16 February, HM Queen Elizabeth II visited Nigeria. On 2 February 1956, XH375 conveyed the Queen during her visit to Enugu, Nigeria. (*Queen's Flight Archive A088*)

HM the Queen and Prince Philip utilised a British European Airways (BEA) Viscount 701, G-ANHE, during a state visit to Portugal on 16 February 1957. (*Portuguese Air Force via Queen's Flight Archives A389*)

The Right Honourable George Ward MP, Secretary of State for Air, greets HM Queen Elizabeth II at RAF Marham on 4 June 1957, ahead of Her Majesty's first flight in a jet aircraft – a Comet T.2, XK669 of No. 216 Squadron, RAF Transport Command – to RAF Leuchars, where she presented No. 43 Squadron with their first colour. (*Crown Copyright/Air Historical Branch image PRB-1-13421*)

The Queen leaving a Comet T.2, XK669 of No. 216 Squadron, at London Airport on 4 June 1957 after her flight back from RAF Leuchars after presenting a new standard to No. 43 Squadron. (*Crown Copyright/Air Historical Branch image PRB-1-16335*)

HM Queen Elizabeth II pictured arriving at Gatwick Airport in Heron C.3 XH375 for the formal opening of the new airport. (*BAE Systems*)

HM the Queen Mother and Princess Margaret at London Airport on 28 October 1958, just about to board BOAC Comet 4 G-APDN. (*BOAC image 19698 via BAE Systems*)

One of the last Royal tours that used Viking C(VVIP).2 VL246 was during the goodwill visit to Nigeria in January 1959. Here, HM the Queen is seen awaiting her transport, having just landed at Lagos on 29 January 1959. (*Crown Copyright/Air Historical Branch image PRB-1-11245*)

The Queen and Prince Philip embark a BOAC Comet 4 at London Airport on 16 June 1959, ahead of a Commonwealth visit to Canada. (*London Airport 19700 via BAE Systems*)

The Queen and Prince Philip, accompanied by Princess Anne and Prince Charles, having just arrived at London Airport on 3 August 1959 on board BOAC Comet 4 G-APDB at the end of their Commonwealth visit to Canada. (*BOAC image 19784 via BAE Systems*)

The Duke of Edinburgh in the cockpit of a Whirlwind helicopter during his visit to Christmas Island in April 1959. (*Crown Copyright/Air Historical Branch image T-916*)

The Duke of Edinburgh's equerry, Squadron Leader John Severne, swings the propeller of Rollason Turbulent G-APNZ at White Waltham on 24 October 1959. It was the Duke's first flight in a single-engine aircraft. (*Crown Copyright/Air Historical Branch image PRB-1-17952*)

At Yeovil, on 5 November 1959, Mr E. C. Wheeldon, managing director of Westland Aircraft Ltd, handed the logbooks of two Whirlwind HCC.8 helicopters – XN126 and XN127 – for the Queen's Flight to Wing Commander R. G. Wakeford. (*Crown Copyright/Air Historical Branch image PRB-1-17989*)

The two VIP Westland Whirlwind HCC.8 helicopters used by the Queen's Flight – XN126 and XN127 – pictured shortly after being handed over at the manufacturer's factory at Yeovil on 5 November 1959. (*Crown Copyright/Air Historical Branch image T-1702*)

Chipmunk T.10 WP903 was allocated to the Queen's Flight in 1960 and remained with the unit for almost three years. After being collected from Silloth in September, it was painted overall fluorescent red. The Chipmunk was originally intended for use by Prince Philip, but was subsequently used to teach the Duke of Kent, Prince Michael and Prince William to fly. Later, it was also used by Prince Charles (*see page 80*). After being withdrawn from RAF service, WP903 was sold onto the civilian market and is now owned and operated by a syndicate based at RAF Henlow as G-BCGC. (*Keith Wilson*)

For the Queen's Asia tour of 1961, it was decided to utilise a pair of venerable Dakota aircraft, especially for the mountainous regions of Nepal. The Queen flew out to India in a Britannia before joining the two Dakota aircraft – KN654 and KN452. KN654 was photographed at Benson ahead of the tour. (*via Michael Prendergast*)

Heron C.4 XR391 of the Queen's Flight at Chester in June 1961, just ahead of its delivery. XR391 was the fourth and final Heron delivered to the Queen's Flight, where it served until retired from service in June 1968. (*Queen's Flight Archive A231*)

Westland Whirlwind HCC.8 XN127 was one of the first of the Queen's Flight aircraft to be repainted in the bright, high-visibility red colour scheme. (*Crown Copyright/Air Historical Branch image T-2845*)

When the Duke of Edinburgh reviewed a passing-out parade at the RAF Technical College at RAF Henlow, on 17 July 1962, he flew himself into the event on board one of the Queen's Flight Whirlwind HCC.8 helicopters. (*Crown Copyright/Air Historical Branch image T-3437*)

The Queen and Prince Philip flew into RAF Scampton on board Heron C.4 XR391 on 10 June 1963, to present a new standard to No. 83 Squadron. They were greeted by the Earl of Ancaster (the Lord Lieutenant of Lincolnshire) and Mr Julian Ridsdale, the Under-Secretary of State for Air, on their arrival at Scampton. (*Crown Copyright/Air Historical Branch image T-5020*)

Hawker Siddeley Andover CC.2 XS790 was handed over to the Queen's Flight on 10 July 1964. (*Crown Copyright/Air Historical Branch image T-8068*)

Just a short while later, the Queen used XS790 to visit RAF Thorney Island on 27 July. (*Crown Copyright/ Air Historical Branch image T-4684*)

Heron C.4 XR391 of the Queen's Flight, pictured during a local sortie from its base at RAF Benson in 1965. (*Crown Copyright/Air Historical Branch image T-5997*)

A typical Queen's Flight scene on the ramp at RAF Benson during the mid-1960s. Left to right are Whirlwind HCC.12 XR486, Heron C.4 XR391 and Andover C.2 XS789. (*Crown Copyright/Air Historical Branch image T-8065*)

Keeping the polished metal finish looking shiny on the two Queen's Flight Andover CC.2 aircraft took a great deal of hard work. However, it later proved to be to the detriment of the aircraft when it was found that the extreme levels of polishing were actually eroding the surface! Later, both aircraft were painted gloss white on the lower fuselage to provide protection for the surface of the metal from the weather. (*Mod image PRB571/29 via Queen's Flight Archives A250*)

One of the Queen's Flight's two Whirlwind HCC.12 helicopters undergoing major maintenance at RAF Benson in 1965. This included suspending the helicopter from the roof of the building and inflating the flotation devices. (*Crown Copyright/ Air Historical Branch image PRB-2-94-0*)

HRH Prince Charles was given a course of air experience flying in a specially painted Chipmunk T.10, WP903, at RAF Tangmere in July and August 1968. His instructor was Squadron Leader Phillip Pinney of the Central Flying School. The purpose of the flights was to examine the Prince's aptitude for flying ahead of a full course of instruction. (*Crown Copyright/Air Historical Branch image PRB-2-345-1*)

The Royal Family chose to utilise a RAF No. 10 Squadron VC10 C.1 aircraft from RAF Brize Norton for their state visit to Brazil and Chile in November 1968 and XV107 was allocated for the task. RAF 'Modification No. 21' introduced all of the alterations to the cabin to accommodate an interior worthy of the VVIP passengers it was to carry. (*BAE Systems*)

The flight crew from No. 10 Squadron chosen to fly the trip gathered outside their VC10 at Brize Norton. (*Crown Copyright/ Air Historical Branch image T-9804*)

Here, a member of the cabin crew demonstrates the luxury of the specially fitted VVIP interior... (*Crown Copyright/ Air Historical Branch image T-9806*)

...while another member of the cabin crew checks the crockery and silver tea pot. (*Crown Copyright/ Air Historical Branch image T-9807*)

The Queen's Flight 1969–95

Beagle Basset CC.1 XS770 was allocated to the Queen's Flight on 27 June 1969 for the Prince of Wales' twin-engine flying training. He completed his first solo flight on XS770 at RAF Oakington on 6 February 1970 (although he was accompanied by his Queen's Flight navigator). When Prince Charles began his Jet Provost course at Cranwell, the aircraft was retained on the Flight to train the Duke of Kent, initially at RAF Leuchars, then later at Benson. It was re-allocated to No. 32 Squadron on 16 September 1971. (*Crown Copyright/Air Historical Branch image PRB-2-859-3*)

During the early part of 1969, the Whirlwind HCC.12 helicopters were grounded following an accident to an RAF Whirlwind HAR.10. In December 1968, the Queen's Flight had 'borrowed' Wessex HC.2 XV726 for crew training in anticipation of the arrival of the Flight's two new Wessex HCC.4 helicopters in 1969.

The first of the new VVIP Wessex HCC.4 helicopters, XV732, was collected from Yeovil on 25 June 1969 and was in Royal use just two days later. The second helicopter, XV733, was handed over on 1 July.

With both Wessex HCC.4 helicopters now in service, the Whirlwind HCC.12s were phased out of use and the last one was flown to No. 15 MU at Wroughton on 23 July.

Beagle Bassett CC.1 XS770 Joins the Flight

Beagle Basset CC.1 XS770 was allocated to the Queen's Flight on 27 June 1969 for the Prince of Wales' twin-engine flying training. After the Prince of Wales began his course on the Jet Provost T.5 at Cranwell, the Bassett was retained by the Flight to train the Duke of Kent at Leuchars and later at Benson. XS770 was re-allocated to No. 32 Squadron on 16 September 1971.

Prince Charles Awarded His Wings

Having flown solo for the first time at Bassingbourn on 14 January 1969, in Chipmunk T.10 WP903, the Prince of Wales eventually made 101 flights in the aircraft before it was finally returned to No. 27 MU at Shawbury on 9 October 1969. The Prince of Wales was awarded his Private Pilot's Licence in March 1969 and an RAF Preliminary Flying Badge on 2 August of the same year. He commenced twin-engine flying in the Bassett CC.1 and after going solo continued to fly the Basset throughout 1970 and 1971. His penultimate trip in the aircraft was to fly into RAF Cranwell on 8 March 1971, when, as a flight lieutenant, he joined the first Graduate Entry at the RAF College to complete his flying training under the auspices of Training Command in Jet Provost T.5 aircraft. Two Jet Provost T.5 aircraft – XW322, coded '1' and XW323, coded '2' – were held at readiness for use by the Prince during his four-month course and both aircraft had the Royal (Prince of Wales) Cypher on the engine intakes. He flew just over 92 hours in the Jet Provost T.5s, 23.5 of them solo, from 8 March 1971. Prince Charles received his wings from Air Chief Marshal Sir Denis Spotswood, Chief of the Air Staff, on 20 August 1971 at the passing out parade at Cranwell.

The Silver Jubilee

In 1977, HM the Queen's Silver Jubilee was a busy year for the Flight. During the year, the Queen made her first helicopter flight when she flew in Wessex HCC.4 XV732 from HMS *Fife* (escort to the Royal yacht) to Hillsborough Castle.

Two Andover CC.2s carrying HM the Queen and HRH the Prince of Wales, along with a Wessex HCC.4 carrying HM Queen Elizabeth the Queen Mother, were utilised with flights to Finningley on 29 July for the Queen's Review of the Royal Air Force.

First Casevac Duties for the Royal Flight

Following the tragic death of Lord Mountbatten in August and the injuries to his family, Lord Brabourne was airlifted from Aldergrove to Northolt, together with his family, on 10 September in Andover CC.2 XS793, which was fitted out for the casualty evacuation (casevac) role – the first time such a role had been undertaken by the Queen's Flight.

Following in his Brother's Footsteps

Prince Edward, following in his brother's footsteps, took up gliding. In July 1980, he attained his Glider Proficiency Certificate at Benson in a Sedburgh TX.1 glider, serial number XN151.

Wings Awarded to Prince Andrew

HRH the Duke of Edinburgh presented Prince Andrew with his pilot's wings at No. 705 Naval Air Squadron on 2 April 1981, at the conclusion of Number 93 course.

'Kitty Four' Crew Arrested

Shortly after the cessation of hostilities in the Lebanon, Princess Anne (President of the Save the Children Fund) visited Beirut while returning from her tour of Southern and East Africa at the end of the year. While on a proving flight during this tour, Squadron Leader Laurie, his crew and the aircraft (XS789) were held on the ground for a number of hours on 18 October 1982 by Zimbabwean troops at Aberdeen 2 airfield, in circumstances very similar to those of Kitty One's incident that had occurred twenty-one years earlier in Mali.

After making contact with the British High Commissioner by relaying a message through an Air Zimbabwe Boeing 707 that was on approach to Harare airport, the captain of the Boeing 707 passed on the message on their behalf. Thirty minutes later, a Swissair DC10 called 'Kitty Four' with a message from the British High Commissioner that read, 'Keep your chins up, we are doing everything possible for you: please call again at 14:00.'

After a further 3-hour delay, a further message was relayed by a Zimbabwean Air Force Britten Norman Islander, advising that 'the problem was about to be resolved'. After thirty minutes, the Zimbabwean Army major returned to the aircraft and informed the crew that as a 'gesture of goodwill', they had been released. They were able to depart and arrived later on the Zimbabwean Air Force ramp at Harare.

New BAe.146 CC.2 Aircraft for the Flight

In 1984, following an extensive evaluation of the BAe.146 at RAF Brize Norton (using ZD695 and ZD696), it was confirmed that the aircraft would replace the Andover CC.2s with the Queen's Flight in 1986. Due to the current and projected tasking, one Andover CC.2 would remain to maintain a total of three fixed-wing aircraft, alongside the two Wessex HCC.4 helicopters.

After completing crew training at Hatfield, the first BAe.146 CC.2, ZE700, was delivered to RAF Benson on 6 May 1986. It was followed by ZE701 on 9 July. The first official flight with the new aircraft was when the Duke and Duchess of York were flown from Heathrow to the Azores for their honeymoon on 23 July; the event was made particularly memorable as the aircraft had 'Just Married' adorned on the air brake for all to see!

Farewell to Two Andover CC.2 Aircraft

With the introduction into service of the two new BAe.146 CC.2 aircraft, two of the Flight's existing Andover CC.2 aircraft were reallocated to No. 32 Squadron at Northolt. XS789 departed on 20 June, with XS793 leaving on 1 October. This just left XS790 with the Flight.

Red Tails for the BAe.146

During the construction and assembly of the BAe.146 CC.2 aircraft, there had been considerable discussion on the colour scheme. British Aerospace was against painting the tail and fin red, claiming the large area would make the aircraft appear tail heavy. Consequently, both aircraft entered service with the Queen's Flight with a while tail and fin. What had not been appreciated during the construction phase was that the red colour on the wings is hardly visible with the aircraft on the ground, due to the anhedral of the wings and their silver leading edges. After delivery, many commented that more red was required for conspicuousness and after much discussion with Buckingham Palace and British Aerospace on the precise colour scheme, the first aircraft was painted with a red fin and rudder in August 1986.

First Royal Tour for BAe.146 CC.2

HRH the Prince of Wales flew to Boston and Chicago from 2 to 6 September 1986. For the trip, the aircraft routed Aberdeen, Reykjavik, Gander, Boston, Chicago/Midway, Goose Bay, Reykjavik and back to Aberdeen.

1987 was the first full year of operations for the two new BAe.146 CC.2 aircraft, during which there were twenty overseas Royal tours, which also involved the Andover CC.2 and Wessex HCC.4 helicopters. All five aircraft completed a total of 989 Royal, Special and VVIP flights during the year.

Fixed-Wing Helicopter PPL for the Duchess of York

The Duchess of York completed her fixed-wing training in a CSE Aviation Piper Warrior, G-BLVL, at RAF Benson. She had made her first solo flight back on 4 November of the previous year and was awarded her Private Pilot's Licence (PPL) in January 1987; she became the first female member of the Royal Family to do so. Later in the year she carried out helicopter flying training in an Air Hanson Bell Jet Ranger, G-DOFY, going solo in October and receiving the PPL (H) license for helicopter flying in December.

Third BAe.146 for the Queen's Flight

In October 1989, it was announced that a third BAe.146-100 was to be purchased for the Queen's Flight, to replace the remaining Andover CC.2, XS790.

On 14 January 1991, the third BAe.146 CC.2, ZE702, was accepted by the Flight. The aircraft had been at Marshall's of Cambridge having the VVIP interior work completed to a standard required by the Queen's Flight. The first task for ZE702 was to fly HM the Queen from RAF Marham to Southampton Airport on 21 January. The last Andover CC.2, XS790, was handed over to the Royal Aircraft Establishment (RAE) at Bedford on 31 January.

Body Blow for the Queen's Flight

On 23 June 1994, the Secretary of State for Defence, the Rt Hon. Malcolm Rifkind, stood up in Parliament and made the following announcement to Members gathered in the House of Commons:

> Following the Efficiency Scrutiny undertaken last year, it has been decided that the Queen's Flight, currently based at RAF Benson, will move to RAF Northolt to join the other Communications aircraft of No. 32 Squadron. Rationalisation into a single co-located unit, which will be known as No. 32 (The Royal) Squadron, will enable the RAF to continue to provide a flexible and cost-effective service to the Royal Family and the other VIP customers. The high standards associated with the Queen's Flight will be fully maintained. The new arrangements will include a centralised tasking and monitoring organisation to ensure the best use of all assets available.

The disbandment of the Queen's Flight and the merger with No. 32 Squadron at Northolt to form No. 32 (The Royal) Squadron took place on 1 April 1995. If the timing was meant as an April Fool's joke, it was in very bad taste! The aircrew, the helicopter support personnel, some service policemen and a handful of engineering manpower transferred to Northolt, although the vast majority of the Flight was posted elsewhere. The engineering support was transferred into civilian hands, to the team who were providing engineering support at No. 32 Squadron. The Captain of the Flight, along with the two Deputy Captains transferred to Northolt and became

Air Equerries with responsibility for ensuring the Royal Family's needs for aircraft were met, but had no command responsibilities within the new organisation.

The Final Months of the Queen's Flight

Although the first three months of 1995 were sad for the Flight, they were also extremely busy for all concerned. Much of the effort was directed towards moving engineering equipment from RAF Benson to RAF Northolt, so that aircraft could remain fully operational during the period of the move. It says much for the Flight that when the aircraft were handed over to the civilian contractors, they were in their usual immaculate condition, despite the BAe.146 aircraft having carried our four overseas tours in March.

The Final Flight

On 31 March 1995, at the end of a visit to the Queen's Flight at RAF Benson by HRH the Princess Margaret, HRH was flown from RAF Benson to Windsor Royal Lodge by Squadron Leader Duggan in Wessex HCC.4 XV732. On departure from Benson, the aircraft conducted a flypast so that HRH the Princess Margaret could wave farewell to the Flight members who were assembled outside the hangar. Sadly, this was the very last flight carried out by the Queen's Flight.

The first Wessex HCC.4, XV732, at Benson, with Whirlwind HCC.12 XR489 in the foreground. After the delivery of both Wessex HCC.4s to the Flight, both Whirlwind HCC.12s were phased out of service and the last was flown to No. 15 MU at Wroughton on 23 July 1969. (*Queen's Flight Archive A1033*)

The Wessex HCC.4
helicopters were very
popular with members
of the Royal Family.
Photographed on
30 September 1970, HM
the Queen Mother was
visiting RAF Kinloss in
one of the Wessex HCC.4s.
(*Crown Copyright/Air
Historical Branch image
PRB-2-1410-14*)

When Prince Charles commenced his course at RAF Cranwell, two Jet Provost T.5 aircraft – XW322, coded '1', and XW323, coded '2' – were held at readiness for use by the Prince during his four-month course. Prince Charles joined the first graduate entry at Cranwell, consisting entirely of post-graduates who had already received preliminary pilot training and who would receive advanced instruction on Jet Provost T.5 aircraft. This air-to-air image, taken in May 1971, shows both of the allocated aircraft in formation. (*Crown Copyright/Air Historical Branch*)

An image of Prince Charles in the cockpit of XW323/2 at RAF Cranwell. Both aircraft had the Royal (Prince of Wales) Cypher on the engine intakes, as can be seen in this image. He flew just over 92 hours in Jet Provost T.5s, 23½ of them solo, from 8 March 1971. Prince Charles received his wings from Air Chief Marshal Sir Denis Spotswood, Chief of the Air Staff, on 20 August 1971 at the passing out parade at Cranwell. (*Crown Copyright/Air Historical Branch image PRB-2-1856-56*)

At the end of his training, Prince Charles visited Strike Command to sample three different types of first-line aircraft under Operation Golden Eagle, including a 2-hour flight in a Phantom FG.1 at RAF Leuchars. Here, Prince Charles is seen being briefed in the cockpit of a Phantom by Wing Commander I. R. 'Hank' Martin, AFC, Commanding Officer of No. 43 Squadron, 19 August 1971. (*Crown Copyright/ Air Historical Branch image PRB-2-1856-40*)

Next stop for Prince Charles during Operation Golden Eagle was to Waddington, where he flew in No. 27 Squadron Vulcan B.2 XL392, although all of the flight crew were from No. 44 Squadron. Prince Charles is seen climbing aboard XL392 under the watchful eye of Flying Officer I. Washington. (*Crown Copyright/Air Historical Branch image PRB-2-1856-131*)

The flight crew and Prince Charles after his flight in Vulcan B.2 XL392. Left to right are: Flying Officer I. Washington; Flt Lt G. Heath; Prince Charles; Flt Lt P. Perry; Flt Lt J. L. T. C. Le Brun (Captain); and Flt Lt P. Marsland. (*Crown Copyright/Air Historical Branch image TN-1-6434-41*)

Prince Charles's final stop was at RAF Kinloss, where he joined the crew for a flight aboard a Nimrod maritime reconnaissance aircraft. He was photographed while in conversation with two flight crew members ahead of his flight on board Nimrod MR.1 XV249 at RAF Kinloss. (*Crown Copyright/ Air Historical Branch image PRB-2-1856-121*)

Throughout Operation Golden Eagle, a 'rescue' Whirlwind HAR.10, XD165, and crew were held on standby. Thankfully, they were not called into action. (*Crown Copyright/Air Historical Branch image PRB-2-1856-105*)

In May 1972, the sad news was announced that the Duke of Windsor had died. As the founder of the Prince of Wales' Flight and later, as Edward VIII, founder of the King's Flight, it was appropriate that on 31 May 1972 his body was flown home from France in a VC10 C.1 of No. 10 Squadron to RAF Benson, where he was laid in state in the station church. (*Crown Copyright/Air Historical Branch image PRB-2-2341-1*)

No. 216 Squadron Comet C.4 XR398 operating a Royal flight into Heathrow on 14 July 1974. (*BAE Systems*)

While attending Gordonstoun, Prince Andrew, the Duke of York, underwent his initial training as a glider pilot during a course with the Air Training Corps at Milltown under Operation Falcon. He was photographed undergoing training on 22 November 1975 in Slingsby T.21B Sedburgh TX.1 WB922. (*Crown Copyright/Air Historical Branch image TN-1-7418-6*)

HRH the Prince of Wales pictured at RAF Wittering ahead of a flight in a two-seat Harrier T.2 aircraft, on 13 July 1977. (*Crown Copyright/Air Historical Branch image TN-1-7706-6*)

In 1977, the Queen made her first helicopter flight when she flew in Wessex HCC.4 XV732 from HMS *Fife* (escort to the Royal Yacht) to Hillsborough Castle. She later returned to HMS *Fife* in XV733 (*seen here*). The following day she flew in XV733 from HMS *Fife* to Coleraine and returned in the same helicopter. (*Queen's Flight Archive A141*)

In 1979, Prince Andrew, the Duke of York, joined the Royal Navy on a short service commission as a Seaman Officer specialising as a pilot. In March he completed his initial pilot training with the Royal Navy Grading Flight at RAF Benson under the auspices of the Queen's Flight. Two Chipmunk T.10 aircraft were allocated for this training, together with a naval instructor, Lieutenant-Commander Sandy Sinclair. (*Queen's Flight Archive*)

Princess Margaret with the Queen's Flight crew and Andover CC.2, which accompanied her on her Royal tour to Swaziland in 1981. A signed photograph was presented to each member of the crew. (*Queen's Flight Archive A1324*)

Above left: Princess Anne arriving at Aberdeen Airport on 17 December 1981 aboard Queen's Flight Andover CC.2 XS790 to join the Royal Family for Christmas at Balmoral. Her dog, however, seems a little unwilling to leave the aircraft and required some assistance! (*Queen's Flight Archive A1306*)

Above right: HM the Queen arriving at the Royal Australian Air Force (RAAF) base at Fairburn on 9 October 1982 aboard a RAAF Boeing 707, during a short visit to open the new National Gallery of Australia. (*Queen's Flight Archive A1139*)

Queen's Flight Wessex HCC.4 XV733 on the lawns outside Balmoral Castle. (*Queen's Flight Archive A1169*)

For some time, the Andover CC.2 aircraft had shown signs of corrosion in the highly polished Alclad skin, particularly on the exposed underbelly. To overcome the problem, all aircraft were painted in a new white polyurethane finish. XS790 was repainted in April 1972 while XS789 (*seen here*) and XS793 followed shortly afterwards. (*Crown Copyright/Air Historical Branch image TN-1-6717-36*)

Classic air-to-air study of Queen's Flight Wessex HCC.4 XV733, photographed over London Bridge. (*Queen's Flight Archive*)

Above left: Prince William made his very first flight aboard a Queen's Flight BAe 146 CC.2 from Kemble to Aberdeen on 17 August 1982. (*Queen's Flight Archive A1197*)

Above right: Andover CC.2 XS790 being repositioned after being dug out of a hole at Njombe Airfield, a grass strip located at high altitude in southern Tanzania. The image was taken in March 1984 during the Prince of Wales' tour. The aircraft started to sink into the soft ground shortly after the Prince had left the aircraft! (*Queen's Flight Archive A1229*)

HM the Queen and the Duke of Edinburgh arriving at Trenton Airport aboard a Convair 580 of the Royal Canadian Air Force (RCAF) on 25 September 1984, a visit to mark the bicentennials of New Brunswick and Ontario. At the time, only Canada, New Zealand and Australia were normally allowed to provide aircraft in which HM the Queen would fly, other than those of the Queen's Flight, British Airways or British Caledonian Airways. The Captain of the Queen's Flight had a duty to advise the Queen on the suitability of any aircraft in which she or any member of the Royal Family would fly. (*Queen's Flight Archive A1134*)

On 26 September 1984, HM the Queen and HRH the Duke of Edinburgh flew to Ottawa on board a RCAF Boeing CC-137 (Model 707) where they were photographed on their arrival. After being introduced to the flight crew, the Royal party went on to meet the welcoming dignitaries. (*Queen's Flight Archive A1126*)

The first BAe.146 CC.2, ZE700, entered production at Hatfield on 30 January 1984 and made its maiden flight on 25 November to Hawarden, where it remained for the completion of its special interior fit. The log book of ZE700 was handed over to the Captain of the Queen's Flight by Sir Austin Pearce, Chairman of British Aerospace, at a ceremony at Hatfield on 23 April 1985. After crew training at Hatfield, the aircraft was delivered to the Flight on 6 May. (*Queen's Flight Archive*)

ZE701, the second BAe.146 CC.2, was delivered to the Queen's Flight on 9 July 1985. (*Queen's Flight Archive*)

On 3 September 1985, Princess Diana visited the BP oil rig *Charlie's Darling*, anchored around 110 miles from the Scottish coast, in the North Sea. She was flown onto the rig by Queen's Flight Wessex HCC.4 XV733. The twenty-four-year-old princess spent 3 hours touring the rig before flying back to the mainland. (*Queen's Flight Archive A1225*)

The Duke and Duchess of York leaving Heathrow on 23 July 1986, bound for their honeymoon. The air brake on the rear of the BAe.146 CC.2, ZE700, had been suitably adorned with 'Just Married'. The aircraft flew to the Azores before the couple joined the Royal Yacht *Britannia*. The trip to the Azores represented the very first official engagement for ZE700. (*Queen's Flight Archive A1283*)

Following her marriage to Prince Andrew, the Duke of York, on 23 July 1986, Sarah Ferguson, the Duchess of York, subsequently became a regular passenger on the Queen's Flight Wessex HCC.4s. (*Queen's Flight Archive*)

Sarah, the Duchess of York, was keen to follow in her husband's footsteps with flying. She commenced flying training in a Piper Warrior, G-BLVL, at Benson. She went solo in November 1986 and was awarded her Private Pilot's Licence (PPL) in January 1987. (*Queen's Flight Archive*)

Not satisfied with a fixed-wing PPL, Sarah, the Duchess of York, commenced helicopter training, once again at RAF at Benson and in an Air Hanson Jet Ranger, G-DOFY. She completed her first solo flight in October 1987 and received the PPL (H) license for helicopter flying in December. She was photographed getting airborne in Bell Jet Ranger G-DOFY at Benson during 1987. (*Queen's Flight Archive A1179*)

A view of the Queen's Flight hanger in late 1986. It contains two BAe.146 CC.2 aircraft (ZE700 and ZE701), an Andover CC.2 and two Wessex HCC.4 helicopters with the Duchess of York's Piper Warrior, G-BLVL, tucked into the left-hand corner. (*Michael Prendergast*)

Flying and Operating with the Queen's Flight

Queen's Flight BAe 146 ZE700 was photographed on 19 November 1994 in the mountainous region of Gilgit, to the north of Pakistan, during a tour of Pakistan and India with the Duke of Edinburgh, who was working on behalf of the World Wildlife Fund (WWF). (*via Steve Hunt*)

Flight Lieutenant Steve Hunt

Flight Lieutenant Steve Hunt joined the Royal Air Force straight from school, in 1978. His officer training was at RAF Henlow and he graduated with the rank of Pilot Officer. His first flying training was on Jet Provosts at RAF Linton-on-Ouse and then on Hawk T.1 s at RAF Valley.

Steve's first squadron was No. 100 Squadron, flying Canberras at RAF Marham and RAF Wyton, where he stayed from 1981 to 1983. He had reached the dizzy heights of Flying Officer by the time he joined No. 100 Squadron.

Then he was appointed as Station Test Pilot at RAF Chivenor from 1983 to 1985 and during this tour was promoted to Flight Lieutenant (a rank at which he remained for the remainder of his career). Then he finally got the tour he really wanted – flying Lightnings at RAF Binbrook, which he did from 1985 to 1988. When the Lightnings were withdrawn from service in 1988, he then returned to RAF Chivenor, flying Hawks as an instructor until 1991.

In 1991 there were only postings to the Tornado F.3 squadrons in the fighter force, as the Typhoon was several years behind schedule entering into service. Consequently, he requested to be posted to No. 32 Squadron at RAF Northolt on HS.125s and, much to his amazement, he actually got posted there in 1991. This posting ultimately led him joining the Queen's Flight in 1994.

Steve had not volunteered to join the Queen's Flight, he had wanted to stay on No. 32 Squadron and complete a second tour as captain on the HS.125. However, one day he was called in to see the squadron commander and told that he was to go to RAF Benson for an interview. The squadron commander advised him that the Queen's Flight required a co-pilot at short notice and wanted someone that they could push through the course quickly.

Steve joined the Duke of Edinburgh's crew, which was captained by Squadron Leader Williams, one of the real characters of the Queen's Flight. The captain, co-pilot, navigator and steward almost always flew together as a crew on whichever aeroplane was allocated, although the crew chief tended to fly 'his' aeroplane regardless of which crew was flying it. 'When we weren't flying the Duke of Edinburgh, we flew any of the other members of the Royal Family that required an aeroplane. At the time, only HM the Queen, the Duke of Edinburgh and the Prince of Wales had their own personal crew.'

Interestingly, Steve Hunt was the very last flight crew member to join the Queen's Flight before it disbanded at RAF Benson and amalgamated with No. 32 (The Royal) Squadron at RAF Northolt.

His tour on the Queen's Flight commenced in May 1994 and he stayed until it disbanded in 1995, when he rejoined No. 32 Squadron upon their amalgamation. Steve Hunt left No. 32 Squadron – and the Royal Air Force – in April 1997 before commencing a career flying executive jets in the Middle East.

Steve Hunt provides a forthright recollection of his time on the Queen's Flight:

The Queen's Flight had been based at RAF Benson for very many years, and was set in its ways. Everything worked like clockwork, so there was little point in changing a winning formula. It was for historical reasons that the crew of the BAe 146 was much larger than that of our civilian counterparts. There was the captain, co-pilot, navigator, crew chief, steward and RAF policeman as a minimum crew every time we had a Royal passenger on board the aeroplane.

The navigator was a hangover from the Andover CC.2 days on the Flight. It was not at all necessary to have a navigator but was felt that they should continue to do the route planning for all the flights, so we continued to fly with one. To be honest, they were brilliant, because they did all the paperwork for each flight and programmed the flight management system in the aircraft. Consequently, they made the life of the pilots very easy. Navigators also tended to be very sociable animals down route, so were also excellent bar companions!

The crew chief was also a hangover from previous aeroplanes when aeroplane serviceability issues were common. However, these crew members knew the aeroplane like the back of their hands and even the slightest problem was usually fixed immediately. Each aeroplane had its own crew chief, who usually flew with his own aeroplane. Once in a blue moon, when there was a serious problem with an aeroplane, the crew chief proved invaluable. While I was on the Royal Flight, not one flight was ever delayed by a serviceability issue, often due to the expertise and knowledge of the crew chief. The crew chiefs were also party animals. It seemed to be a prerequisite for the job. Many a morning I regretted trying to keep pace with them in a bar the night before.

Only one steward was carried regardless of the number of passengers. Consequently, they either had a very easy job, or could be rushed off their feet.

The policeman was carried, ostensibly to guard the aircraft while it was on the ground. During a day trip he always stayed around the aeroplane. However, any time we had a night stop, he was with us in the hotel. I never did quite fathom out how he guarded the aeroplane from the comfort of a downtown pub!

On flights that were away from base for a week or longer, several extra engineers were also carried on board. This meant we had an engineer who covered engines, airframes, avionics and electrics. So on a long 'Tour' away from base, it was not unusual to have a crew of nine or ten. This meant we had an instant party when we landed in some weird third-world backwater. Life was very sociable on the Royal Flight, even in the most remote regions of the world.

The value of the on-board engineering support can best be demonstrated when we consider one particular incident. We had embarked on a three-week tour of the Far East. After leaving RAF Northolt, we suffered a generator failure. We were planning refuelling stops in both Malta and Luxor, en-route to a night stop in Bahrain. Using our second radio we called our base and arranged for a spare generator to be flown out to Bahrain that evening. The generator arrived on a British Airways flight the same evening, and our crew chief and extra engineers replaced it and ground-ran the aeroplane overnight so that we were fully serviceable again in the morning. The passengers never even know there had been a problem and no delay to the itinerary occurred. This was when the engineers really earned their money.

The navigator would do the planning for a Royal flight and a NOTAM (Notice to Airmen) would be issued for the 'purple airspace' around our flight. Purple airspace was restricted and controlled airspace around the route of the flight and the NOTAM was designed to warn other pilots to keep well away from the Royal aeroplane. The purple airspace was valid for a period of fifteen minutes before the planned flight time until thirty minutes after the flight had planned to pass. Sadly, this system has now been scrapped and is no longer in use.

When it was time to go out to the aeroplane and get it ready for flight, the pilots literally just walked into the cockpit and sat down. The crew chief had done everything by the time the pilots arrived – the external inspection and the internal checks. The navigator had already programmed the flight management system. The only thing left to do for the flight crew was to press the engine start buttons!

Most Royal flights started and ended from either RAF Northolt or Heathrow Airport. Consequently, the initial flight from RAF Benson was usually empty to position the aircraft before the passengers arrived. At the end of the day there was usually another empty leg back to RAF Benson.

One of the biggest benefits of having either a member of the Royal Family or the Prime Minister onboard was that there was never a delay caused by airport or air traffic restrictions. We were given priority over all other traffic, except medical or in-flight emergencies. So, when Joe Public in his airliner got a forty-minute delay (and occasionally much longer) on the tarmac, we never had to worry about whether we would be allowed to depart on time.

The easy part was the actual flight. The passengers were, without exception, wonderful. Every member of the Royal Family was always a pleasure to fly. They seemed to relax on board the aircraft when they knew that no one could bother them until they were back on the ground. They were always incredibly polite to the crew and most of them had a great sense of humour, which regularly came to the fore when they were chatting to us up on the flight deck. Likewise with the Royal Protection Officer from the Metropolitan Police Force, who would always accompany the passenger. They too could relax with the crew knowing that for the duration of the flight, the passenger was totally safe from the outside world.

Flying the aircraft was the easy part of the day. All the hard work had gone into preparing for the trip. The major difference between the ways the Royal Air Force fly compared with the airlines is that we put the safety and comfort of the passengers ahead of saving money or generating profit. So, for example, we never flew the steep noise abatement profiles on take-off because that may have been uncomfortable and probably spilt the coffee. We always tried to arrive at the destination within a couple of seconds of the planned arrival time. Invariably there would be a huge welcome committee and sometimes a flypast that was due overhead the moment we opened the doors. Consequently, we flew whatever speed we required to make our arrival time accurate, regardless of the ideal fuel economy speed. We also planned our descent so that we didn't need to use the airbrakes, which may have caused a vibration in the cabin area and therefore caused the G&T to slop around the glass. Engine power changes were also kept to an absolute minimum so that the passengers could not detect any variation in engine noise. A perfect flight consisted of just six movements of the throttles: full power for takeoff; climb power after takeoff; cruise power; idle for the descent; the power setting for the approach with the wheels and flap down; and idle as you crossed the runway threshold. Any more throttle movements and it meant you had not flown the ideal flight profile. Then, once back at base it was time for tea and medals at the end of another hard day at work!

There were about six or seven major 'tours' around the world each year, which involved an aircraft complete with a full crew travelling to an area of the world with one of the senior members of the Royal Family on board.

The most popular tours with the crews were usually to the USA or South America. However, I much preferred the Far East. All the pilots were on a waiting list for the major tours and when they reached the top of the list they were put on the next tour. After the tour, they went back to the bottom of the list. When I reached the top of the list, I would turn down a tour to the Americas or Russia, stay at the top of the list and wait for a more exotic Far Eastern tour. This was how I got my first major tour, which was to Pakistan and India with the Duke of Edinburgh, who was working with the World Wildlife Fund.

For my final big Royal tour, I once again waited at the top of the list until another Far Eastern trip arrived. This time it was to Hong Kong, Vietnam, the Philippines and Indonesia with the Duke of Gloucester, accompanied by many heads of British industry. It was for a full three weeks – what a great way to end my RAF career. I was crewed with my Flight Commander, who was the deputy boss of the Squadron. He was also due to leave the RAF the following month, so it was going to be a swan song for both of us. We were going to take the Duke of Gloucester plus many heads of British industry on a huge sales tour of the Far East. There was literally going to be many millions of Pounds' worth of exports at stake on this trip.

At the end of the trip the Duke and the industry representatives thanked all the crew personally for helping the sales tour prove such a success. Many export orders worth hundreds of millions of pounds had been signed in each country. The CBI had paid for the cost of using the aeroplane, but the cost paled into insignificance when compared to the value of the orders received. It was a huge loss to British industry when the Queen's Flight was disbanded and the Royal Yacht decommissioned.

Personally, it was a very sad day when the Queen's Flight disbanded.

The 'official' crew picture of the World Wildlife Fund tour to Pakistan and India in 1994, signed by the Duke of Edinburgh. (*Crown Copyright via Steve Hunt*)

The crew of ZE700 photographed at Gilgit, all suitably adorned with the local head attire. Steve Hunt is on the far left of the picture. (*via Steve Hunt*)

The 'official' crew picture of the World Wildlife Fund tour to Madagascar and South Africa in 1995, once again signed by the Duke of Edinburgh. As President of the WWF, the visit to Madagascar enabled Prince Philip to help in the protection of endangered lemurs in Madagascar. He then joined the Queen in South Africa for a Commonwealth summit, wherein South Africa re-joined the Commonwealth, which it had left back in the early 1960s. It was the Queen's first visit to South Africa since 1947, when she had visited with her father, King George VI. (*Via Steve Hunt*)

Another crew picture, this time featuring local Vietnamese head attire, during the 1995 tour with the Duke of Gloucester and members of British industry that included a stop in Vietnam. (*via Steve Hunt*)

An overnight stop with No. 32 Squadron at Sarajevo on 19 February 1996 required some extreme measures from the crew to clear the snow. (*via Steve Hunt*)

No. 32 (The Royal) Squadron at RAF Northolt on 9 June 1996, shortly after the disbandment of the Queen's Flight and its incorporation into the squadron. Steve Hunt can be seen in the second row, second from the left. In the background of the image are the various aircraft and helicopter types operated by the squadron at the time. (*Crown Copyright/32 Squadron via Steve Hunt*)

Royal Flying Since 1996

An interesting air–to-air photographic sortie was flown by No. 32 Squadron on 29 May 2002, just a couple of years before the striking red tail and flying surfaces were re-painted white. It featured one of the squadron's BAe 146 CC.2 aircraft, ZE700, leading a pair of BAe 125 CC.3 aircraft – ZD620 and ZE396. (*Crown Copyright/Air Historical Branch image MNT 020-60-002*)

When The Queen's Flight merged with No. 32 Squadron, the new unit was renamed No. 32 (The Royal) Squadron – although this is sometimes presented as No. 32 (TR) Squadron). Along with the merger, all of the former Queen's Flight fleet of three BAe.146 CC.2 aircraft, and a pair of Wessex HCC.4 helicopters were transferred to Northolt.

Since the merger, the BAe.146 CC.2 aircraft have been in transport service within several recent theatres, including Operation Granby (during the Gulf War), Operation Telic (Iraq in 2003) and Operation Veritas (activities in Afghanistan), as well as in the Balkans, Sierra Leone, Libya, Mali and Somalia.

The biggest impact of the merger was the effective ending of dedicated VIP flights in RAF transport aircraft. Officially, the aircraft of No. 32 Squadron are available to VIP passengers only if they are not needed for military operations. This was officially declared in 1999, with the Ministry of Defence (MoD) stating:

> The principal purpose of 32 Squadron [is] to provide communications and logistical support to military operations; the Squadron's capacity should be based on military needs only; and any Royal or other non-military use of ... spare capacity is secondary to its military purpose.

History of No. 32 Squadron

No. 32 Squadron was originally formed on 12 January 1916 at Netheravon and was equipped with Henry Farman F.20 aircraft in May of the same year. The squadron saw action during the First and Second World Wars, being equipped with fighter aircraft, but was disbanded on 3 February 1969 while operating Canberra B.15 aircraft at Akrotiri, Cyprus.

On the same day No. 32 Squadron was reformed at RAF Northolt when the Metropolitan Communications Squadron was re-designated. At the time it was involved in VIP flying and over the next twenty-five years or so operated an interesting mixture of aircraft and helicopters, including the Pembroke C.1, Sycamore HC.14, Bassett CC.1, Andover CC.2, Whirlwind HCC.12, HS.125 CC.1, CC.2 and CC.3 variants, Andover C.1 and Gazelle HCC.4 helicopters. Some of the airframes it operated had previously served with the Queen's Flight.

On 1 April 1995, No. 32 Squadron merged with the Queen's Flight, effectively bringing all of the RAF's communications assets into one location, including the three former Queen's Flight BAe.146 CC.2 aircraft. The merger did spell the end of the RAF's dedicated VIP transport aircraft as, according to a statement from the Royal Air Force:

> Number 32 (The Royal) Squadron's role today is Command Support Air Transport (CSAT) - the movement of small groups of high priority personnel or cargo by air in order to facilitate global key leadership engagement and further UK influence. The Squadron is tasked to deliver a safe, secure and responsive CSAT capability for senior military commanders, Government Ministers and occasionally the Royal Family.

RAF Board of Enquiry on Royal Flight BAe.146 Released

On 29 June 1994, while still being operated by the Queen's Flight, a BAe.146 CC.2 was involved in an accident at Glenegedale Airport, Islay, in the Hebrides.

On 19 July 1995 it was announced that the Prince of Wales had given up piloting Royal flights following the crash, in which a Queen's Flight BAe.146 CC.2, ZE700, was damaged to the tune of £1 million. St James's Palace announced the Prince's decision as an RAF Board of Inquiry found that the aircraft captain had been negligent in allowing him to take the controls. Prince Charles was not blamed because, despite holding the RAF rank of Group Captain, he was regarded as a passenger who was invited to fly the aircraft. The RAF Board of Inquiry can only pass judgment on the crew.

The RAF report into the accident, released in the House of Commons on 18 July 1995, concluded the jet was flying 32 knots too fast when it crossed the runway threshold. Only 509 metres of the 1,245-metre-long runway remained when the aircraft touched down, nose wheel first, with a 12-knot tailwind component. It is understood that the wheel brakes were then applied 'before the full activation of the anti-skid protection systems', causing both inboard main wheels to lock and the subsequent failure of their tyres. There were no reported injuries.

The RAF Board concluded that the captain of the aircraft, Squadron Leader Graham Laurie, was negligent in that '[he failed] to intervene when the aircraft performance and limitations were exceeded in the final stages of the flight'. The navigator was also apparently found 'negligent' for 'failing to advise the captain of the tailwind component and to draw his attention to the inaccurate approach parameters'.

Distinctive Livery Disappears

In 2004, the MoD conducted a review into the distinctive colour scheme of the BAe.146 CC.2 aircraft of No. 32 Squadron's aircraft inherited from the Queen's Flight. Concern had been voiced in some quarters over a potential vulnerability to terrorist attack as a result of their distinctive red colours. Although defensive countermeasures had already been fitted to all three of these aircraft, it was decided to remove the bright red colours entirely, thereby offering a more civilian airline-look about them while, hopefully, lowering their profile.

Agusta A109E Helicopters Join No. 32 Squadron in 2006

In May 2005, a contract was awarded to Agusta Westland to provide No. 32 Squadron with three Agusta Westland A109E helicopters to replace the three Twin Squirrel helicopters then in use with the squadron. The initial contact was for a five-year period, commencing on 1 April 2006, although it was later extended on 31 March 2011 to allow two of the A109Es to continue in squadron service for a further year.

Former Queen's Flight Wessex HCC.4 Helicopters Preserved

When the pair of former Queen's Flight Wessex HCC.4 helicopters were delivered to RAF Northolt on 1 April 1995, they joined the operations of No. 32 Squadron. When No. 32 Squadron ceased to provide helicopter operations for the Royal Family, their role was effectively replaced with a Sikorsky S-76 operated by Air Hanson, awarded by the Royal Household. Both HCC.4s were moved into storage at RAF Shawbury in 1998, where they remained until eventually being offered for preservation.

XV733 was delivered by the Royal Navy to the Helicopter Museum at Weston-super-Mare on a low-loader on 15 November 2001. XV732 was moved by road to the RAF Museum at Hendon, where it was delivered on 26 March 2002.

Additional BAe.146 Aircraft for No. 32 Squadron

In March 2012, the decision was taken to acquire a further two BAe.146 aircraft for No. 32 Squadron. The contract was awarded to BAe Systems and two second-hand series 200QC aircraft (QC for Quick Change) were acquired from TNT Airways. They were extensively overhauled and re-fitted for their new military tactical freight and personnel transport role by Hawker Beechcraft. Both aircraft were designated BAe.146 C.3 and were delivered in a flat grey colour scheme in April 2013, where they were quickly placed into squadron service, initially in the Afghanistan theatre.

Farewell to the BAe.125

On 16 March 2015, when No. 32 Squadron's last BAe.125 C.3 returned from operations in Afghanistan, it heralding the types retirement from the Royal Air Force. Of the final four operational aircraft operated by the squadron at the time of retirement, three were put up for sale and one (ZD621) was place on permanent display at RAF Northolt. The aircraft were retired from service seven years ahead of their original anticipated withdrawal date.

Air Transport of the Royal Family and Government of the UK

Following the merger of the Queen's Flight in 1 April 1995, alternative arrangements were made for the carriage of members of the Royal Family and the Government of the UK, depending upon circumstances and availability, utilising a variety of military and civilian operators.

These include the Queen's Helicopter Flight (part of the Royal Household), No. 32 (The Royal) Squadron, chartered civil aircraft, but most often by scheduled commercial flights, with the Royal Family normally choosing to fly with British Airways.

Nowadays, most flights taken by Government ministers are on board scheduled airline flights. The MoD's position is currently that the use of aircraft from No. 32 Squadron is recommended 'only when there is not a more cost-effective solution with the commercial sector or where security arrangements dictate that special flights should be used'.

New Voyager Available for VVIP Use

In November 2015, at an estimated cost of £10 million, the UK Government proposed a VVIP upgrade to one of the RAF Voyager aircraft. At the time, ZZ336 was one of fourteen Airbus A330MRTT Voyager aircraft being operated by the AirTanker Consortium under the Future Strategic Tanker Aircraft (FSTA) contract. This private finance initiative had originally been announced by the Government in January 2004, with fourteen new Voyager KC.2 and KC.3 aircraft replacing both VC10 and Tristar tanker aircraft then in RAF service.

Once upgraded, the aircraft could also be used for ministerial flights as well as for members of the Royal Family. As a consequence, many charter flights would no longer be required, providing a saving of around £775,000 a year. The new VVIP plan was expected to cost around £2,000 per flying hour for the A330MRTT, compared with an estimated £6,700 per hour for long-haul charter.

The £10 million refit costs included a secure satellite communications system, a defensive missile detection system and seating for 158 passengers. After conversion, ZZ336 retained its RAF all-over grey livery and continues to operate in its primary air-to-air refuelling role when not required as a VVIP aircraft. It was first used in this VVIP role on 8 July 2016, when it flew Government ministers from London to the 2016 NATO conference in Warsaw.

Royal Household and the Queen's Helicopter Flight (TQHF)

Up to March 1997, the responsibility for travel by the Royal family had been shared by the Ministry of Defence, the Department of Transport and the Foreign and Commonwealth Office. However, on 1 April, it was transferred to the Royal Household, with funding provided by the Department of Transport. In the same year, the Royal Household was given authorisation to acquire a helicopter for its private use and the Queen's Helicopter Flight (TQHF) was created.

The TQHF is part of the Queen's Private Secretary's department of the Royal Household, and is the organisation tasked by the Royal Travel Office at Buckingham Palace. Initially, from 1998 to 2009, it used a single Sikorsky S-76C+ twin-engine helicopter, painted in striking maroon colours and registered G-XXEA; the registration was chosen in honour of Airspeed Envoy G-AEXX, the aircraft that the Queen's uncle, the Prince of Wales, first flew in the King's Flight.

G-XXEA entered service on 21 December 1998. The S-76 is a commercial helicopter operated widely around the world, usually with a crew of two and seating for up to thirteen occupants in the cabin. The Queen's helicopter is only fitted with six seats to provide additional comfort.

G-XXEA was withdrawn from service in October 2009 and sold in the USA. On 28 September 2009, a new, upgraded Sikorsky S-76C++ helicopter, G-XXEB, was delivered to TQHF and remains in service today.

Cpl Paul Farmer, one of two Arms and Explosives Search Dog Handlers on No. 32(TR) Squadron Air Transport Security Section. The unit has two dogs: Cocker Spaniel 'Monty', and 'Jess', a brown and white German Short Haired Pointer, who were photographed at work in one of the squadron's aircraft. (*Crown Copyright/Air Historical Branch image NHT-05-204-8438/SAC Smith*)

Following the death of Diana, the Princess of Wales, in France on 31 August 1997, she was flown back to the UK on 1 September aboard a No. 32 Squadron BAe.146 CC.2, ZE702. Her coffin was draped in a Royal Standard after being removed from the aircraft at Northolt and placed into a hearse. (*Crown Copyright/Air Historical Branch image NHT-32SqnHistorical-510*)

HRH the Duke of Edinburgh landing at RAF Leuchars for Prince William's graduation from the University of St Andrews on 23 June 2005. (*Crown Copyright/Air Historical Branch image LEU-05-0765-0004/SAC Insley*)

Station commander Group Captain J. D. Maas greets Her Majesty the Queen and the Royal Corgis on their arrival at RAF Northolt in 2005, having flown in aboard a No. 32 Squadron BAe.146 CC.2. (*Crown Copyright/Air Historical Branch image NHT-07-253-6129/SAC Ryan Onody*)

No. 32 Squadron BAe.146 CC.2 aircraft ZE701 was photographed at Northolt on 13 June 2015. This aircraft, a former member of the Queen's Flight, was repainted soon after moving to No. 32 Squadron as the high-visibility red was considered a high risk when the aircraft is in theatre. (*Keith Wilson*)

Spectacular air-to-air photograph of No. 32 Squadron BAe.146 CC.2 ZE700 over Oxfordshire, taken during formation practice with another of the squadron's aircraft – a BAe 125 CC.3. The formation practice was ahead of both aircraft participating in a major flypast. (*Crown Copyright/Air Historical Branch image NHT-107-124-2228/ Cpl Dylan Browne*)

Another No. 32 Squadron BAe.125 CC.3, ZD704, outside on the ramp at Northolt on 18 December 2012 during a special photographic 'night shoot'. (*Keith Wilson*)

The VVIP interior of a No. 32 Squadron BAe 125 CC.3. (*Crown Copyright/Air Historical Branch image NHT-20120628-0190-0013/SAC Neil Chapman*)

No. 32 Squadron Agusta A109E ZR322 at the special 'night shoot' at RAF Northolt on 18 October 2012. This was one of three A109E helicopters operated by the squadron on lease from the manufacturer, Agusta SPA. (*Keith Wilson*)

The third Agusta A109E helicopter leased from the manufacturer for use by No. 32 Squadron was ZR323, photographed at RAF Northolt on 7 June 2008. (*Keith Wilson*)

When the lease of three helicopters reached its initial period, only one helicopter – ZR322 – was retained for use by No. 32 Squadron. However, when ZR322 underwent major servicing at RAF Syerston, G-CDVB (the former ZR321) was leased from Agusta Westland as cover. It was photographed at RAF Northolt on 13 June 2015 during the station's 'At Home' Day. (*Keith Wilson*)

In addition to the former Queen's Flight BAe.146 CC.2 aircraft, No. 32 Squadron also operated two of the C.3 variant – ZE707 and ZE708. The C.3 is the civilian equivalent of the series 200QC (QC for quick change). ZE707 (*seen here*) was purchased on the second-hand market, where it had previously operated as F-GLNI and OO-TAZ before being rebuilt to the RAF's specifications. It was photographed at RAF Northolt on 13 June 2015. (*Keith Wilson*)

HRH Prince William underwent basic flying tuition in the Grob Tutor T.1 with No. 1 Elementary Flying Training School at RAF Cranwell. He was photographed at the controls, in company with his instructor, on 14 January 2008. (*Crown Copyright/Air Historical Branch image CCT-08-004-0020/Cpl Scott Robertson*)

After completing the EFTS course, the next stop for HRH Prince William was the Tucano T.1. On 18 February 2008, he was photographed in ZF485, in formation with ZF292, somewhere over the Lake District. (*Crown Copyright/Air Historical Branch image CCT-08-004-0029*)

HRH Prince William made the transition to helicopter training with the Defence Helicopter Flying School at RAF Shawbury, during his four-month time with the RAF. HRH is seen here at the controls of a CFS Squirrel over the Welsh mountains on 25 March 2008. (*Crown Copyright/Air Historical Branch image CCT-08-004-0048/Cpl Scott Robertson*)

HRH Prince William alongside his helicopter instructor – Squadron Leader Allison – at No. 60(R) Squadron, the RAF element of the Defence Helicopter Flying School at RAF Shawbury, on 11 March 2008. (*Crown Copyright/Air Historical Branch image CCT-08-004-0041/Cpl Scott Robertson*)

Flying Officer William Wales at the controls of a C-17 Globemaster during his visit to RAF Brize Norton on 14 April 2008. (*Crown Copyright/Air Historical Branch image CCT-08-004-0083/Cpl Scott Robertson*)

On 17 April 2008, HRH Prince William joined a No. 101 Squadron VC10 at RAF Brize Norton. While airborne, the Prince took to the controls and later watched the VC10 aircraft air-to-air refuel fighter aircraft, as well as watching the VC10 being refuelled aloft. (*Crown Copyright/Air Historical Branch image CCT-08-004-0107/Cpl Scott Robertson*)

On 23 April 2008, HRH Prince William visited RAF Coningsby, where he was given an opportunity to fly in the rear cockpit of a No. 29 Squadron Typhoon T.1 aircraft. (*Crown Copyright/Air Historical Branch image DPR-2199*)

Prince William receives his wings from his father, Prince Charles, during a presentation ceremony at RAF Cranwell on 11 April 2008. (*Crown Copyright/Air Historical Branch image DPR-08-24-026/Sgt Graham Spark*)

Flt Lt William Wales, the Duke of Cambridge, was posted to No. 1564 Flight, Mount Pleasant Complex, on the Falkland Islands. He was photographed on 4 February 2012 while conducting a pre-flight check on Sea King HAR.3 XZ491, ahead of a search and rescue sortie. (*Crown Copyright/Air Historical Branch image MPC-20120204-061-011/ Sgt Andy Malthouse ABIPP*)

Flt Lt William Wales, the Duke of Cambridge, preparing for a flight in Sea King HAR.3 XZ591 with No. 1564 Flight, Mount Pleasant Complex, on 4 February 2012. (*Crown Copyright/Air Historical Branch image MPC-20120204-061-016/ Sgt Andy Malthouse ABIPP*)

HM the Queen and the Duke of Edinburgh paid a visit to RAF Valley on 1 April 2011, where their grandson, the Duke of Cambridge, was undergoing training with the Search and Rescue Flight (SARF). (*Crown Copyright/Air Historical Branch image SAR-11-143-081/SAC Dek Traylor*)

HM the Queen shares a light-hearted moment with her grandson, the Duke of Cambridge, during her visit to RAF Valley on 1 April 2011. (*Crown Copyright/Air Historical Branch image SAR-11-143-OUT-UNC-173*)

Like his older brother Prince William, Prince Harry took up flying, but with the British Army. Captain Wales served a twenty-week deployment to Afghanistan during the winter of 2012/13, in the cockpit of a British Army Apache. Harry helped to launch the Invictus Games in 2014, and remains patron of its Foundation. He left the army in June 2015. (*Crown Copyright/Air Historical Branch image 45158776*)

In 1998, HRH the Duke of Edinburgh visited an aircraft company in North Yorkshire, where he arrived on board Sikorsky S-76C helicopter G-XXEA, operated by the Director of Royal Travel. The registration was chosen in memory of the famous Royal Airspeed Envoy 3 G-AEXX. G-XXEA returned to the USA in 2009. (*Keith Wilson*)

HRH the Duke of Kent, Patron of the RAF Charitable Trust, seen departing the Royal International Air Tattoo at RAF Fairford in a Sikorsky S-76C-2, G-XXEB, after visiting the event on 17 July 2011. G-XXEB is registered to the Keeper of the Privy Purse, the Queen's Helicopter Flight. (*Lee Barton*)

HM the Queen departing RAF Northolt aboard a BAe.146 Series 200 of Cello Aviation on 17 May 2011, en route to Ireland. G-RAJJ is regularly chartered by members of the Royal Family. (*Crown Copyright/ Air Historical Branch image NHT-11-0163-0046/Cpl Wayne Beeching*)

On 15 July 2015, a team from the Joint Aircraft Recovery and Transportation Squadron (JARTS), based at RAF Wittering, carefully lowered No. 32 Squadron's last BAe.125 CC.3, ZD621, into its final resting place alongside the squadron's main ramp and hangar at RAF Northolt, being preserved as a reminder of the type's lengthy and valuable service with the squadron. (*Phillip Dawe*)

On 12 January 2016, No. 32 Squadron celebrated 100 years of RAF service and they painted these special markings onto BAe.146 CC.2 ZE700 to celebrate the occasion. ZE700 was photographed at Northolt on 12 January 2016, shortly after the aircraft left the hangar having just had the special markings applied. (*Lee Barton*)